The Wide World of Aaron Burr

The Wide World
of
AARON BURR

by Helen Orlob

The Westminster Press

Philadelphia

Library of Congress Catalog Card No. 68–11032

Published by The Westminster Press®
Philadelphia, Pennsylvania

Printed in the United States of America

CONTENTS

CHAPTER 1

"THAT AARON!"

IN THE OLD CEMETERY at Princeton, New Jersey, where so many of Princeton University's distinguished dead are buried, a tall, white shaft marks the grave of a man whose name has long been fought over in the pages of American history. Weathered by more than a century, and abused by the crude tools of the curious, the monument bears a dignified epitaph that conveys no hint of the storms of controversy aroused by the man who lies beneath it. It reads:

AARON BURR
Born Feb. 6th 1756
Died Sept. 14th 1836

A Colonel in the Army of the
Revolution

Vice-President of the United
States from 1801 to 1805

The stone, plainly more recent than those surrounding it, was cut in New York at Brown's marble yard in

1856. When the order came to the yard, the stonecutter scratched his head. "Aaron Burr," he read. "That's funny. The fellow's been dead for twenty years. Why did they wait all this time for a stone?"

"Likely the family was afraid of vandalism and didn't want the whole world to know where he was buried," said the foreman. "You remember who he was?"

"For a fact, I do. Murdered Alexander Hamilton, didn't he? And wanted to be an emperor in the West? I'd forgotten that he was Vice-President. Never knew, I guess."

Then, as later, most people knew very little more than did the stonecutter about Aaron Burr and the role that he had played in the founding of the republic. The brilliant youth, the courageous officer, the eminent officeholder who had been a United States senator and Vice-President had been forgotten. Almost nothing about him had survived but the memory of a man so loathed as a murderer and a traitor that he had been obliged to flee the country.

Esther Burr, who lies close to her son in Princeton cemetery, would have grieved had she lived to know this. Still, she might not have been surprised, for she seems to have glimpsed the man her two-year-old son would become: *Aaron is a little, dirty, Noisy Boy very different from Sally in everything,* she wrote. *He begins to talk a little, is very Sly and mischievous. He has more sprightliness then* [sic] *Sally & most say he is handsomer, but not so good tempered. He is very resolute & requires a good Governor to bring him to terms.*[1]

Unerringly, Esther Burr had singled out factors that

were to be dominant in the formation of her son's character and personality: He was handsome, she said, lively, self-assertive, determined, capable of mischief and intrigue. She had seen the need for control. Neither she nor her husband lived to provide it. Aaron Burr's story would perhaps have been different had his parents survived a few years longer.

Princeton University provides a beginning as well as an ending to an account of Burr's life. He was not yet a year old when his father, president of the College of New Jersey, brought his family from Newark to Princeton, where the school had been relocated. The Reverend Burr must have been proud to show his wife the spacious president's house and the fine, new building, soon to be named Nassau Hall, for they were largely the products of his own efforts in planning and fundraising. He must have been happy and confident of the future too. The little college, which eventually assumed the name of the village, was growing, and Mr. Burr loved teaching even better than the ministry. Unfortunately, his future was of short duration. Ten months later he died of an illness brought on by exhaustion.

Esther Burr's father, the famous Puritan preacher, Jonathan Edwards, was named to his son-in-law's post, and tragedy continued to stalk the family. Only a few months later, father and daughter died of smallpox within days of each other. Esther's mother proposed to adopt the orphaned children, two-year-old Aaron and his four-year-old sister, Sally. Shortly, the grandmother, too, was carried to the little cemetery in Princeton. Aaron had lost all of those who had been close to him. One of them might well have been the "good governor" whose need his mother had fore-seen.

For the next two years he and Sally were cared for by family friends in Philadelphia. Then Esther's brother assumed their guardianship. Timothy Edwards had been cast in his father's mold. He was stern, self-righteous, unyielding. Much that happened later was to prove that he loved his sister's children dearly, but the expression of affection for a small boy, particularly one so trying as young Aaron, was beyond him. According to Uncle Timothy's lights, warmth of feeling could not be mixed with education in the Christian virtues. During the years that he spent in the Edwards household in Elizabethtown, New Jersey, Aaron was constantly at odds with his uncle.

He must have been there only a short time when he first tried running away. "I think I stayed out three or four days that time," he remembered, telling stories of his childhood long afterward. It was not to be the last escapade of the sort, in spite of the fact that Mr. Edwards' punishments were not easily forgotten. There was one in particular that Aaron Burr still clucked over in old age. It was administered on a July day that should have left an eight-year-old boy only happy memories of warm sunshine and ripe cherries, high in a tree. Presently, on that afternoon, an ancient lady flounced into Timothy Edwards' study. "That boy of yours," she cried. "That Aaron! He thought I wouldn't see him up there, throwing cherries at me. My dress! See what he's done!" She thrust the stained folds of her silk skirt at Timothy.

"I could always tell how bad the beating was going to be by the length of the sermon and the prayer that preceded it," Burr reminisced. "They were long that day. He licked me like a sack."

There was another story of his boyhood that Burr liked to tell too. At the age of ten, he again took to his heels. This time he would go to sea, he resolved, and the stern uncle would see no more of him. He made his way from Elizabethtown to New York. A tiny, slight figure, even for his years, with delicate features, pale skin, and flashing black eyes, he must have been an odd sight as he walked the docksides, searching for a berth aboard one of the big sailing ships.

Still, he was not long in finding a captain to listen to the earnest story of an orphan whose uncle no longer needed him. The captain, liking the appearance of the lad and his straightforward manner, signed him on as cabin boy. It happened that the ship was not to sail for several days, and some acquaintance of the Edwards family who had business on the waterfront reported Aaron's whereabouts to Timothy. He set out to recapture the rebel.

When the boy recognized his uncle advancing toward the ship, he scrambled up the shrouds to the masthead. "Aaron!" Timothy shouted, pointing to the deck. The boy shook his head with determination. The crew gathered, the captain explained, Timothy continued to shout, and Aaron remained mute and defiant. "I knew he wasn't going to come up there after me, and I figured that as long as I could hang on, I was safe," said Burr. "At last, my uncle decided to open negotiations. 'No licking, if you come down,' he promised. 'We'll forget about this episode.' An indefinite future on the masthead had no appeal for me, and I finally agreed to come down and go home with him, hoping that in some fashion things in Elizabethtown might take a turn for the better."

Happily, Aaron's affairs did improve upon his return. A new tutor, Tapping Reeve, was engaged for both the Burr children. This young man, later a distinguished lawyer and jurist who became Aaron's brother-in-law, proved to be a great friend. He earned the boy's devotion at once by pointing out a new means of escape from the household. "You learn well, and you are advanced for your years," Reeve told his pupil. "If you work hard, you should soon be ready to enter college."

Aaron took fire at the idea, and worked furiously for a year. Presumably, at the end of the period he was competent in the Greek and Latin college entrance requirements, for pupil and tutor came to Timothy Edwards, requesting that the boy be permitted to try for admission to Princeton. "Ridiculous!" said Timothy, but the two persisted, and at last he granted them leave to go down to the college for an interview.

President John Witherspoon echoed Timothy Edwards' sentiments and dismissed them shortly. "You may be the son of a distinguished president of the college and the grandson of another who was his equal, but that will make no difference to me," he told Aaron. "College life is not for babies. It is for young men. Come back when you are grown."

Reeve was crestfallen. Aaron was enraged. "I'll show him," he resolved.

Two years later, at thirteen years of age, an inch or two taller, a few pounds heavier, Aaron Burr again presented himself at Princeton. "I have completed all the work of the freshman and sophomore years," he

informed Dr. Witherspoon. "I want to enroll as a
junior." The arrogance of his manner must have been
insufferable, but the truth of his assertion could not be
denied. A brief examination proved it.

Nevertheless, a thirteen-year-old junior was no more
acceptable than an eleven-year-old freshman. "You
may enter as a sophomore, not as a junior," the president decreed. Aaron argued, but to no purpose. Witherspoon remained adamant. The boy entered the
College of New Jersey as a sophomore.

During his first year he continued to be as indus-
trious as he had been under Reeve's tutelage, studying
sixteen to eighteen hours a day. However, the year-
end examinations proved such diligence to be unneces-
sary. Aaron Burr was found to be far in advance of
his fellows. Thereafter, in normal schoolboy fashion,
he worked only as hard as he must. He graduated with
honors in the fall of 1772 at the age of sixteen.

Burr had by that time reached his full growth. He
was five feet, six inches tall and made the most of
every inch with the erect bearing of a soldier. A por-
trait painted shortly after he left Princeton shows a
handsome youth, dark-haired and black-eyed, with
a determined mouth and a firm chin. The face is re-
laxed in a pleasant expression — the artist has only
hinted at the captivating smile and brilliant eyes
which friends and enemies alike were later to consider so remarkable.

The Princeton years were important to Burr for the
friendships he made there. His classmates, Matthias
Ogden and William Paterson, were to be devoted to
him throughout their lives. Samuel Spring remembered him long afterward, in the time of disgrace, not

only as a college friend, but as a superbly courageous soldier.

There were enemies of the future at Princeton, too — James Madison the most notable. There is no record of association between the two during the college years but, later, when they became bitter political enemies, they cannot have failed to remember each other as youths.

Burr, at sixteen, was reluctant to leave the college environment. He had enjoyed its stimulation, and he was not ready to make a decision on his future, in spite of the advice that poured upon him from all sides. " The Burr and Edwards families have both produced famous clergymen," said his friends and teachers. " You cannot ignore this tradition."

The period during which he pondered their counsel was one of the happiest of Burr's life. Often, in the spring and summer following his graduation, he was in Elizabethtown with Matt Ogden. Together, they explored the countryside and spent long days on the water, poling and sailing every stream and bay of the nearby Jersey shore. They yarned the pleasant hours away, gossiping a bit about the Elizabethtown belles who were plainly finding handsome little Burr so attractive a companion. It was a fascinating subject — the girls were charming. But for Burr, the crucial speculation of the moment had to do with the shape of his future. Should he try the ministry, he asked Ogden, or should he heed the dictates of his skepticism and forget it?

At last, in the fall of 1773, he made up his mind. " I shall go to visit Dr. Joseph Bellamy," he told Timothy Edwards. " If he thinks there is any hope for me and will have me, I'll study with him."

Edwards was overjoyed. He could not imagine a teacher better able to deal with a difficult seventeen-year-old than Bellamy, who had been Jonathan Edwards' pupil. The Bellamy home in Bethlehem, Connecticut, had become a sort of theological seminary, and when Burr was accepted into the household, his uncle was sure that the boy would, at last, be all right.

His confidence was misplaced. The youth stayed in Bethlehem only a few months. Far from being a docile student, he proved to be a doubter who questioned the tenets of Christian doctrine with cool intellectualism. "The road to Heaven is open to all alike," he decided eventually, and bade his instructor good-by. Dr. Bellamy must have seen him go with a certain amount of relief.

"I had the good doctor completely under my thumb," [2] Burr told one of his friends with malicious delight.

Aaron Burr never thereafter discussed his religious beliefs with anyone. During his later life he attended church frequently, as became a man in the public eye, but it is thought that he was a Deist (a person who, believing in a Creator, holds no strong convictions on Christian doctrine).

Tapping Reeve, his former tutor, had by this time married Sally Burr and was practicing law in Litchfield, Connecticut, a short distance from Bethlehem. Burr had often been their guest during the months at Dr. Bellamy's. Now Reeve urged him to consider the law as a profession. "Come stay with us," he invited. "You can read law under my supervision."

Burr consulted his uncle. "It is a matter of indiffer-

ence with me," said the discouraged guardian. " I
would have you act your pleasure therein." ³

It pleased the young man to accept Reeve's offer
and, in 1774, he began to read law, as happy a field
of endeavor for one of his disposition as theology had
been unhappy. Moreover, burgeoning ambition and a
taste of the delights of worldly living had ruled in favor of the legal profession.

Litchfield society proved to be as gay, the young
ladies as diverting, as had been the case in Elizabethtown, and Burr set out to win hearts with zest. He was
rumored to be engaged, and Ogden wrote to know if
it were true.

The news is groundless, his friend replied. *It is so
far from being true, that scarce two persons can fix on
the same lady to tease me with.*⁴ Indeed, Aaron Burr
had no intention of saddling himself with a wife at
that stage of his career. When an uncle of whom he
was very fond urged the merits of an alliance with an
attractive heiress, he sidestepped the issue as best he
could.

*I am determined never to have any dealings with
your friend Cupid until I know certainly how matters
will turn out with you,*⁵ he wrote Ogden who had
lately confessed himself in love. Should that romance
end, continued Burr, *in such a case, I say, I would
choose to be untied, and then, you know, the wide
world is before us.*⁶

CHAPTER 2

BENEDICT ARNOLD'S
VOLUNTEER

THE "WIDE WORLD" should have been three years
in the future for a student who had just embarked
upon a course of reading law, but there is a hint in
Burr's words to Ogden that he had already glimpsed
the possibility of a more active life. Like all of his
young countrymen with a taste for adventure, he was
taking a deep interest in the current of excitement that
was sweeping through King George the Third's American colonies.

In fact, every post that reached Litchfield made it
appear more likely to Burr that he would be a soldier
before he became a lawyer. Delegates had been summoned to a Continental Congress at Philadelphia to
urge upon His Majesty the rights of his overseas subjects. Boston, rebelling against unreasonable taxation,
had put on a "tea party," and in the towns and villages men were storing arms. The Reeve lawbooks
gave way to volumes of military history against a day
that seemed inevitable.

That day came, at last, in April, 1775, and Burr re-
sponded to the news of Lexington and Concord with
the eagerness of a youngster hearing fire bells. *Join me*

here, he begged Matt Ogden. *We must volunteer at the start.* Burr thought, as did most people, that the struggle would be brief, and it was characteristic of him to want to be on the scene when the plums of leadership were distributed.

Willing enough but less impetuous, Ogden said that it would take some time to settle his affairs. June brought the news of the Battle of Breed's Hill (Bunker Hill), and Burr could contain himself no longer. " I'm going to Elizabethtown and prod Matt into action," he told Sally and her husband. He scarcely listened to their protests concerning his youth and slight physique as he prepared to leave.

Early in July, Burr and Ogden reached Cambridge, Massachusetts, where American recruits were gathering to oppose the four thousand British regulars stationed in Boston under General Thomas Gage. They bore a letter of introduction from John Hancock, who had known Burr's father, to General Washington: *This will bring to your attention Aaron Burr and Matthias Ogden, two young gentlemen of the Jerseys.*

If Burr had thought that such a letter would win him instant favor with Washington, he was mistaken. The general, in the first days of his command, was too engrossed with the problems of making a fighting force of some fifteen thousand ill-clad, undisciplined, and largely unarmed recruits to pay more than scant attention to such recommendations. It is not known that he even saw the " two young gentlemen of the Jerseys."

Burr probably resented the snub, and it may well have marked the beginning of the contempt and dislike for Washington that he felt all his life. Even in old age, Burr's bitterness toward the long-dead leader had not abated. His first biographer remembered that he wanted to include in his reminiscences a condemnation of Washington as both soldier and statesman.

In any event, Burr and Ogden were given no assignment, although they were commissioned as officers. They wandered about the camp, Burr increasingly disgusted with what he saw. Officers, many of them unfit for command, had little control over the recruits. Virtually no attempt was being made to police the filth of the place, and the resulting illnesses were assuming epidemic proportions. Burr, himself, was shortly bedridden with a fever of some sort. " Disgust has sickened me as much as anything," he told Ogden.

One day, while he lay in bed, reflecting angrily on the sacrifices he had made to join a do-nothing, ragtail mob, he overheard Ogden talking with a number of men nearby. The word " expedition " was repeated several times. " Arnold has said he will leave shortly," someone remarked, as the group broke up. " If he does, the journey could be made before bad weather sets in."

" Matt," Burr called out. " What expedition are you talking about? "

Ogden entered the tent. " It's to be a move on Quebec," he began and broke off with alarm when he saw the expression on his friend's face.

" Go on. Go on," Burr urged.

" Now, look here, old boy, don't start getting notions about this. Do you have any idea how far across Maine it is to Quebec? "

" That's to be the route, is it? " Burr boosted himself

up in bed. Impatient questions tumbled from his lips. "Who is to command? What kind of force? What's the plan?"

"General Washington figures to drive the British from their Canadian bases and, perhaps, gain an alliance with Canada. General Schuyler is heading one force that will move on Montreal by way of Lake Champlain. Colonel Benedict Arnold will command the expedition to Quebec. It's to be a volunteer force of eleven or twelve hundred, and he's asking for hardy types — woodsmen and hunters." Ogden shot a significant glance at his friend's slight frame.

Burr began reaching for his clothing. "You fool!" Ogden cried. "This expedition is going to travel almost six hundred miles through a wilderness. Only a few men have ever made it through Maine to Canada. Montrésor, a British officer, did it fifteen years ago, and he barely got through alive."

"The route must be along the river courses," Burr reflected. "That's the only way it could be done."

"Montrésor showed that on his map — up the Kennebec to the Dead River, follow the Dead to its source, then cross the mountains to the Chaudière which flows into the St. Lawrence opposite Quebec." Ogden had been eyeing Burr with increasing alarm. "It may sound easy, but it won't be. The healthiest of us will have a hard time and, for you, it would be impossible."

"Pshaw, I'm as fit as the next man," said Burr. "All I need is some good reason to get out of this bed." He shrugged into his clothes, tottering with weakness. Once, Ogden had to steady him.

Burr soon made it clear that nothing would keep

him from joining the expedition to Quebec, and his health improved swiftly. On September 14, 1775, he shouldered a pack and set out for Newburyport, some sixty miles distant, where Arnold's troops were staging. The journey seems to have done him no harm, for, on arrival, he was his usual cocky self.

Timothy Edwards had not been consulted when his nineteen-year-old ward decided on the military adventure. " The young idiot! " he cried, on learning that Burr had ridden off to the wars. " This will be the end of him if I don't put a stop to it." He dashed off a letter, ordering his return. " Find him, give him this and bring him back — if you can," he instructed a messenger. Then, he sighed. " I am very well acquainted with Aaron's disposition, and I really doubt that you will be successful. I had better write another. Give it to him if he will not accompany you."

Burr had reached Newburyport before the messenger caught up with him. The young officer glanced at Edwards' demand coolly, knowing that he was now beyond his uncle's power to command. " How do you expect to take me back if I should refuse to go? " he asked. " If you were to make any forcible attempt upon me, I would have you hung up in ten minutes."

The envoy stuttered a moment or two. Then he said, " Very well, I have done my best. Mr. Edwards did not really expect you to return with me. He sent this also." He gave Burr a packet that contained a gift of money and the second letter, an expression of affection and an entreaty to abandon the expedition to Quebec, lest it prove to be too much for his frail health. Burr shook his head and smiled a little as he pocketed the gift.

Late in September, at Fort Western (now Augusta, Maine), Arnold's force embarked upon the Kennebec in some two hundred clumsy, scowlike boats that had been slapped together of green pine timber in a space of two weeks. Almost at once it became apparent that the river would be no easy highway. Boatmen who had set out to row or pole the wretched craft upstream were soon obliged to leap over the sides, hauling and pushing through shoal water. At times waist-deep, they were carried off their feet by swift currents, whereupon their boats went careening into rocks that ripped planking and opened badly calked seams.

It was not long before the boats were left to the crews who had them in charge. The rest of the men took to the shore, preferring the ordeal of thrusting through brush and timber to that of being half drowned most of the time. Burr, however, remained on the river, putting to good use the skill in boat-handling that he had learned at Elizabethtown. Apparently, he was in the best of health, for no one ever noted that he was sick, nor did he seem to suffer greatly from the hunger that was added shortly to the other trials of the journey.

Dr. Isaac Senter, expedition surgeon, first realized, only ten days' travel from Fort Western, that Arnold's army might be facing starvation. Making his way down the river to observe the progress of the boats, he had seen many of them battered to wreckage and had examined their cargoes with mounting horror. Most of the precious provisions they carried had been ruined by water. "We have very little but salt pork and flour left," he told Arnold.

At Fort Western the boats had been laden with forty-five days' provisions. Had all gone well, that would have been enough. However, by the time the expedition began to toil across the miles-long portage from the Kennebec to the Dead River, many days behind schedule, almost half the food had been lost. Rations were cut to a minimum.

The weather was frightful. Freezing nights followed days of incessant rain, and men slept in clothing frozen " a pane of glass thick." Shortly, snow began to frost the ground. So many men fell sick that Arnold was obliged to order a blockhouse built for those who could not continue.

The " young gentlemen of the Jerseys " tightened their belts with the rest, Ogden limping along on cloth-bound feet, while Burr, the youth whose friends had known he could not survive the journey, seemed to gain a measure of strength from adversity. Colonel Arnold noted and was to remember in dispatches Burr's spirited conduct throughout the expedition.

Montrésor's map had been shown to be inadequate or mistaken on a number of occasions, but its most disastrous fault was not revealed until Arnold's men, struggling down from the Appalachian crossing, found themselves in a wild country of snow-laced swamps, precipices, and ravines. Streams wandered in every direction, and there was not a clue to tell the companies which one might lead to Lake Megantic, source of the Chaudière River.

At this point, the food supplies gave out entirely. Men ate roots grubbed from the frozen earth, tallow candles, the boiled hide of moccasins, a starving dog that had been their companion. They died and were

left where they lay for want of the energy required for
burials.

At last, after days of wandering in a wilderness that
is still virtually impenetrable, the survivors staggered
out on the lakeshore. Arnold pressed on in haste with
a small company, and a short time later, sent back
supplies from Canadian settlements to the tattered
scarecrows of his command.

With renewed strength and determination, the rem-
nants of the expedition, barely more than five hundred
men, continued the march down the Chaudière and,
on November 7, they stood at last on the banks of the
St. Lawrence, gazing across at the heights of Quebec.

The element of surprise had been lost, for Arnold's
advance had been well-reported, but the miserable
Americans at the river's edge still counted upon success. "Just wait until Montgomery brings his men
down the river," said an officer. "Then, we'll have the
place, and all Canada too!" (General Richard Montgomery, who had replaced Philip Schuyler, had already taken Montreal.)

The enemy had thought to hold the invading force
on the far side of the St. Lawrence by destroying all
the boats there, but the job had not been well enough
done to defeat the Americans. The river bank was
scoured, upstream and downstream, for leaky old tubs
that could be patched up for a crossing, and when
Montgomery appeared a few days later with three
hundred men, Arnold's force was encamped beneath
the fortress wall.

Plans for the attack were weighed by a council of
officers, and Burr, outranked by virtually everyone,
succeeded in making himself heard. "An assault upon

the walls by means of scaling ladders would be completely unexpected," he claimed. " With a few diversionary attacks, we could take the place quickly." His superiors agreed that the scheme might work, ladders were built, and Burr plunged into training exercises with fifty men. Then the plan was abandoned as too risky. Instead, a two-pronged attack was to be made upon the Lower Town. The forces were to unite there and push their way into the citadel.

On New Year's Eve, 1775, in the midst of a blinding snowstorm, Arnold moved on Quebec from the east while Montgomery's men clambered over snow-covered hillocks of ice on the river shore, west of the city. Aaron Burr, who had been named a captain and aidede-camp to the general, was at his side. Heads down against the vicious wind, muskets held close, the attackers crept through a narrow passage toward a blockhouse. British soldiers, celebrating the year's end in traditional fashion, saw the advancing column tardily and fled the fortification. Quick success was within Montgomery's grasp until one of the enemy, more clearheaded than the rest, turned back to fire a cannon shot that alerted nearby defenders to the danger.

" Push on, brave boys, Quebec is ours! " [7] the general shouted. A hail of musket fire poured into the passage. Montgomery fell, mortally wounded, and one by one, men around him toppled. Only Burr and a guide remained on their feet. " Push on! Push on! " Burr cried, echoing the fallen leader's words.

The column, irresolute for a moment, began to move again. Then there was a thin cry from the rear: " Retreat! Colonel Campbell says fall back! " Montgomery's second in command had given up without a fight.

The men whom Burr might have rallied turned and ran, leaving him alone beside the body of his general. Samuel Spring, who had gone as chaplain to the expedition, saw him there, stooping in the snow to shoulder Montgomery's body, and staggering a few steps with it. Then, " the General being a large man, and Burr small, and the snow deep," [8] he put it down, Spring remembered long afterward. Aaron Burr has been accused of many things, but no one has ever called him a coward.

Arnold's force, on the other side of the town, soon found trouble too. Early in the assault, the colonel's leg was shattered by a musket ball. "We are sold," men whispered to each other, seeing him supported to the rear. Nevertheless, under Captain Daniel Morgan, they moved forward, fighting from street to street. At the point where Montgomery was to have joined him, Morgan continued the battle, but when the British surrounded his position, he was forced to surrender. The attack on Quebec was over. More than half of the Americans who had taken part in it were dead, wounded, or captives.

Arnold, still in command despite his wound, decided to lay siege to the city. It was a costly tactical error, for Quebec, awaiting reinforcements that were bound to come, had little to fear from an enemy preyed upon by disease, hunger, and the bitter cold of the Canadian winter.

Burr, promoted to brigade major for bravery during the attack, was disgusted with the inactivity of the siege, and he was disillusioned with Arnold. After a few weeks he had no thought but to get away. It has been charged that the young major deserted Arnold in order to return to the colonies, but this is not so. When he left Canada in April, Burr wrote his sister, Sally, *I go on Public Business,*[9] making it clear that he had been resourceful enough to find a legitimate excuse for leaving the miserable camp on the St. Lawrence.

CHAPTER 3

MAJOR BURR CONTRIBUTES HIS MITE

DURING THE EARLY SPRING of 1776, while Benedict Arnold maintained his hopeless position before Quebec, the American siege of Boston was drawing to a successful conclusion. After Washington fortified the heights of Dorchester in March, the British fled the city by night. At once the general began to move troops south to New York in order to defend Manhattan Island whose possession the Congress regarded as vital to the American cause.

The Mortier Mansion on Richmond Hill, in the present Greenwich Village, was selected as headquarters, and there Washington started to plan his defense. The tempo of the war was about to quicken, staff work was increasing, and there was a need for young officers at Richmond Hill. So it happened that Major Aaron Burr, newly returned from Canada, and recommended for brilliance and ability, was appointed to the headquarters staff. Late in June, 1776, he climbed, for the first time, the steps of the splendid house that was, one day, to be his own.

One may only speculate on this brief interlude in the Burr story. Very little is known about it beyond the widespread rumors of dissension between Washington and his new aide, who was said to have offered the Commander in Chief counsel from his freshly acquired fund of military lore. It was probably Burr of whom the general spoke when he remarked that he had enough trouble without being forced to "listen to beardless boys spout their ideas of military tactics." At any rate, the young man took his leave of the official household after only a week or so.

His next post suited him much better. Named an aide to General Israel Putnam, Commander of the American forces in the New York area, he was accepted into the general's family, which included his wife, daughters, and a lovely young British hostage who promptly lost her heart to the handsome major. The assignment, promising a taste of active warfare and a chance to flirt with a pretty girl, was more in Burr's line than duty in the stiff formality of Washington's household at Richmond Hill.

During the summer of 1776 the British began landing troops on Staten Island, preparatory to an attack on New York City. Washington sought to deny the enemy an advantageous position on Long Island by stationing a large portion of his army on Brooklyn Heights. Soundly defeated in the Battle of Long Island, August 27, the Americans retreated to Manhattan Island in a gale of wind and rain.

Burr had observed the troops on Brooklyn Heights, knew that they were not fit for battle, and was scornful about plans for a defense of New York City. "This is madness," he claimed. "The city should be burned to the ground and left to the British."

Washington had reason enough, however, for his

decision to make a stand on the island. For one thing, Congress was insisting on it. For another, American morale was so low after the defeat on Long Island that the Commander in Chief feared his army might disappear in the course of another retreat.

On September 14, the British made a landing on the eastern shore of Manhattan about four miles above the city. The defenders, largely untrained country boys, fled before the brilliant ranks of the enemy with scarcely a backward glance. Washington, raging at their cowardice, knew that he must move swiftly to save almost three thousand men, stationed in the city, who might now be cut off from the main force. " Give the order to evacuate," he told General Putnam. " Move the troops north to Harlem Heights as fast as possible."

All during the next day, while the British general, Sir William Howe, dawdled unaccountably on his beachhead, American soldiers moved out of New York City, hustled along by officers who could not doubt that at any moment the enemy might start to cross the island, cutting off the escape route. Late in the day, Colonel Henry Knox, temporarily in command of a brigade, was sure that it had been cut. He turned back to a fort on a slight rise known as Bunker's Hill.

Major Aaron Burr, who had seen enough action that day to satisfy even his restless spirit, rode up. " What are you doing here? " he cried, aghast at finding troops holing up in the fort. " Who is in command? " Knox growled a reply. " Why haven't you retreated with the rest? " Burr demanded.

" Impossible," said Knox. " The enemy are across the island. I'm going to defend this fort."

"That's nonsense," Burr snapped. "You can't defend yourself without provisions or water. And there is a way open — I can guide you."

"It would be insanity," the colonel shouted.

The brigade officers had been standing by, taking in the hot words between Knox and the handsome youth sitting his lathered horse. Burr turned to them. "If you stay here, you'll all be crammed into dungeons or hung up like dogs. I'll get you out of this place — better that half should be killed fighting than that all should end as cowards. Are you with me?"

The brigade, deaf to the colonel's sputtering indignation, was with Burr, and he led the way along obscure paths and roads to the safety of Harlem Heights. Knox must have had a thought for his own reputation, for he failed to report the young officer's insubordination, and the incident went unmentioned in dispatches.

(It is said that another officer named Alexander Hamilton was in Knox's brigade that day. If this was the case, it may be that Hamilton first saw Burr, his mortal enemy, as a brash youngster engaged in relieving a superior of command.)

On the following day, in the Battle of Harlem Heights, the Americans routed a British advance and knew an initial taste of victory in that insignificant action. Burr must have seen, as Washington did, that with troops thus inspirited, an orderly withdrawal would be possible.

While the British general again dawdled at strengthening his positions on the island, the American forces faded into the hills of Westchester. September's heat gave way to autumn chill. Burr felt the cold and wrote to Sally, asking her to send buttons from his old clothing so that he could have cloth made up. *He wanted a Pr. of Leather Drawers & two Pr. of the coarsest of my Winter Stockings too.*

Again the British came up, attacking at White Plains, New York, at the end of October. Defeated, the Americans fell back into New Jersey, and as winter drew on and despair mounted, Washington continued to retreat, pursued by the enemy. Congress fled to Baltimore when Philadelphia was endangered, and Burr accompanied Putnam to prepare defenses for the capital.

That Christmas in Pennsylvania was dreary, but a few days later there was amazing news that the tide of defeat had been halted at the Delaware. Washington had crossed the river on a savage Christmas night that must have reminded Arnold's veterans of New Year's Eve, 1775. Trenton, New Jersey, had been taken from the stupefied British and their Hessian allies. A week later, it was reported that Princeton, too, had fallen.

The British began a hasty withdrawal to the safety of New York, and Washington led his exhausted men into winter quarters at Morristown, New Jersey. Congress returned to Philadelphia, while Putnam's force moved north to mop up in the wake of the astounding victories.

The unhappy Burr, whose notions of his proper role in warfare had ill accorded with supervising pick-and-shovel work on city defenses, was given another distasteful assignment: The general set him to quizzing prisoners for information. Increasingly fretful and restless, he was still at it in Princeton two months after the town had been taken.

The major was having to swallow a number of bitter pills at the time, and not the least of them was the fact that Matt Ogden had long since achieved the rank of colonel. Burr longed for command, but was obliged to write Ogden: *As to " expectations of promotion," I have not the least, either in the line or the staff. . . . But, as I am at present happy in the esteem and entire confidence of my good old general, I shall be piqued at no neglect. . . . 'Tis true, indeed, my former equals, and even inferiors in rank, have left me.*[10] He had had *assurances from those in power*, he continued, but he would not stoop to jog their memories. The letter ended with a mealymouthed expression of humility that was sheer hypocrisy: *We are not to judge of our own merit, and I am content to contribute my mite in any station.*[11]

Undoubtedly, Burr did not know that others were being promoted over his head because he had been too loud and too bold on a number of occasions. For instance, it is likely that he had enraged Washington with offers of military advice, and he had certainly ridden roughshod over the authority of Henry Knox who was now close to the Commander in Chief, and would have no good word to say for him.

Washington was not the man to let irritation and personal prejudice influence his thinking, however. He had recognized in " little Burr " qualities that he could not afford to ignore in any man. Burr must be employed more usefully. In the summer of 1777, he was promoted to lieutenant colonel, with orders to report to the regiment of Colonel Malcolm at Ramapo, New Jersey.

The Commander in Chief received a most unusual

acknowledgment of the promotion: *Burr was truly sensible of the honour,* he wrote. *I am nevertheless, sir, constrained to observe, that the late date of my appointment subjects me to the command of many who were younger in the service. . . . I would beg to know whether it was any misconduct in me, or any extraordinary merit or services in them, which entitled the gentlemen lately put over me to that preference?* He continued by asking *whether I may not expect to to be restored to that rank of which I have been deprived?* [12] If there was an answer, Burr did not preserve it.

CHAPTER 4

COLONEL OF THE MALCOLMS

THE TRANSFER TO MALCOLM'S REGIMENT was more significant than Burr's orders had indicated. Colonel Malcolm, a New York merchant without military experience, had raised the regiment, and finding himself unable to deal with any of its problems, had asked Washington for an officer to assume command.

"This youngster will never do," he told himself when the twenty-one-year-old stripling reported, but within a few days, he had changed his mind. "You shall have all the honor of disciplining and fighting the regiment, while I will be its father," [13] said Malcolm and, forthwith, moved from the camp. He was seldom seen after that.

The authority of a regimental commander fit Burr like a well-tailored coat. Malcolm's green recruits found themselves toeing the mark for a stern disciplinarian who was, nevertheless, just and considerate. Years later, when Aaron Burr, disgraced and ruined, applied for a Revolutionary pension, some of them spoke up in his favor. Said one veteran, "It was Burr who formed it [the regiment], and it was a model for the whole army in discipline and order. . . . His

attention and care of the men were such as I never
saw, nor any thing approaching it, in any other officer,
though I served under many." [14]

During the late weeks of summer, while Burr
worked with his new command, distressing news of
enemy activity filtered into Washington's headquarters: An army, under " Gentleman Johnny " Burgoyne,
was on its way south from Canada, using the same
route by which Montgomery had advanced in 1775.
Another, commanded by Barry St. Leger, was march-
ing east through the Mohawk Valley. Succeeding
dispatches did nothing to raise American spirits: Fort
Ticonderoga, on Lake Champlain, had been lost. Burgoyne was nearing Albany. Only the force under General Horatio Gates stood between a meeting of the two
British armies there.

The only hopeful aspect of the picture was the evidence that General Howe had no intention of forming
the third prong of the offensive with a thrust north
on the Hudson from Manhattan Island. Howe had
sailed away with his troops, destination unknown.

Washington knew that he could not go to Gates's
aid. He must be prepared to counter a powerful strike
by Howe at some point on the coast, and he set his
staff to casting up totals of available strength. Orders
went out to commanders, among them General Putnam, directing them to hold in readiness for immediate action whatever units they could spare.

Such top-level planning was not for regimental ears,
and Burr could not have known that his men were
among the fifteen hundred counted upon from Putnam. The Malcolms were coming along nicely — their

firebrand colonel meant to seek action at the first opportunity.

Early in September, hard-riding couriers brought him news of an enemy foraging expedition near Hackensack, a mere thirty miles distant. Within an hour, Burr had secured the camp and was on the march with his three hundred men. A messenger, sent express from Putnam's headquarters, came pelting after him with orders: *Get your regiment and the public stores into the mountains immediately.*

Burr flipped away the message and wrote a cool refusal: *I cannot run away from an enemy whom I have not seen. I will be responsible for the public stores and for my men.* Clearly, the reply stemmed from his conviction that he was a better judge of the situation than his superior.

Men have been court-martialed for less, and that might have been Burr's fate, had he met with disaster. However, less than twenty-four hours after leaving camp, he surprised the enemy guard and, with the aid of hastily organized militia units, promptly routed the main force of twenty-five hundred men.

Burr would have gone in pursuit, but again there was a courier from Putnam. Possibly this time the orders made sense to the young man. General Howe had landed at the head of Chesapeake Bay. He was threatening Philadelphia, had crossed the Schuylkill. Washington needed reinforcements on the line in Pennsylvania. Once more, Malcolm's regiment took to the road.

Information on its employment for the next few weeks is vague. It is not known whether Burr saw action during the American defeats at Brandywine Creek and Germantown, Pennsylvania, which sealed Philadelphia's fate, but he was certainly with the main army in the dreary weeks that followed, when the results of the battles were tallied.

Washington's officers refought the fog-shrouded action at Germantown endlessly, clucking over "what might have been," and as they did, triumphant news from the north drifted in, bit by bit: St. Leger was retreating in the Mohawk Valley. Burgoyne had surrendered to Gates at Saratoga, New York. There were thousands of prisoners. The British menace from Canada had been wiped out.

What had the men in Pennsylvania to contemplate in the face of such tidings? Theirs was a beaten army, huddled in tatters twenty miles from the capital it had striven to defend. Their general had had to accept defeat, while Gates was riding herd on a captured army. A little group of malcontents among the officers drew from these facts a false conclusion: Gates was the better man and should be named Commander in Chief. As the army trailed into winter quarters at nearby Valley Forge, General Thomas Conway, an Irish troublemaker, assumed the leadership of an intrigue to relieve Washington of command.

Gates was not the only man mentioned in the secret councils at Valley Forge. A number of the plotters, among them Aaron Burr, thought that the logical choice to succeed Washington might be his second in command, Major General Charles Lee, who boasted of vast military experience in Europe, and had sneered at his superior as "most damnably deficient." At the time, he was a prisoner in Philadelphia, but they urged consideration of his name, should he be exchanged. Had Lee's partisans known how much he was enjoying captivity, and how intimate he had become with General Howe, they might have had some second thoughts about their man.

Conway believed that Congress would need only a little prodding to see the wisdom of a change. Some of the delegates were unhappy with Washington's record, while others, like John Adams, had confessed themselves uneasy about the devotion which the general had earned. They feared that he might eventually become the founder of a ruling dynasty.

In the autumn of 1777, Congress should have concerned itself with its own shortcomings, rather than with those imagined in its general. The commissary and quartermaster departments that it had set up to supply the wintering army were proving to be almost useless. The small quantities of food sent to the bleak camp on the Schuylkill River dwindled to nothing. Clothing, shoes, and blankets failed to appear. As the weeks passed, hunger, nakedness, filth, and disease mounted with an appalling toll. It is estimated that twenty-five hundred men died at Valley Forge during the winter of 1777–1778.

Washington chose to ignore the plotting against him, of which he was fully aware, and bent all his efforts toward relieving the sorry condition of his troops. At times it seemed to him that the army would never survive the winter for anyone's command.

The gloom at headquarters during the black misery of those months thinned a little, however, after visitors began to talk of a possible alliance with France. A pair of newcomers in the camp cheered the Commander in

Chief too. The Marquis de Lafayette, young, buoyant, and dedicated to the cause of American freedom, had joined his staff, and the Baron von Steuben, a professional soldier from Prussia, had ridden up, bearing a commission from Congress to train the ragged volunteers into some semblance of a proper army.

February's ice and snow still lay upon the camp when von Steuben first glimpsed the scruffy horde that he had promised to tutor. His fat Teutonic face stiffened with horror. Never had he seen an army like this one. But he set to work, shouting in a ridiculous hash of German, French, and English at ragged lines that were daily reduced by disease and death. For a time, it appeared that he had undertaken an impossible task. Nevertheless, he persisted, and as winter gave way to spring, Washington could see the results. The Baron was creating a military force quite unlike the one that had fought the battles of 1776 and 1777.

At last, in May, when the German drillmaster deemed his pupils ready for graduation exercises, there was added reason to celebrate with a great review. Three months earlier, Dr. Benjamin Franklin had signed a pact with France. Help was on the way — a French fleet, under Admiral d'Estaing, had already sailed westward.

Shortly thereafter, news of the alliance and resulting seaborne threat reached Philadelphia, where Sir Henry Clinton had replaced Sir William Howe. Clinton was now obliged to consider that his position was none too safe. Suppose d'Estaing were to appear off the capes of the Delaware? With Washington at his back, Clinton would be cut off from the New York base. A siege and eventual capitulation were not impossible. The British general decided to get out of the city quickly.

Late in June, Washington's intelligence informed him that the enemy had begun to evacuate Philadelphia. Here was a chance to strike a blow with his revamped army — a flank attack on an enemy burdened with supplies and strung out along the line of march. Some of the American officers were doubtful about committing the main strength of the army to the undertaking. "What will happen if the British turn to encircle us?" they asked, and supplied a defeatist answer: "The war would be over, in spite of our new allies."

Major General Charles Lee, exchanged for a British general, had swaggered back into camp, sure as ever that only he was fit for the top command. "Americans will never stand up to British grenadiers," [15] said he in the council, and was seconded by several of the more timid officers. His edict brought black looks from the younger men, and Washington cocked an inquiring eye at Anthony Wayne. "Fight, sir!" [16] said Wayne. Lafayette, Nathanael Greene, and others nodded with vigor.

"We will march," Washington decided finally, and no matter what his feelings might have been about Charles Lee, was obliged to ask him to lead the action. Lee declined contemptuously. "The assignment is a more proper business of a young, volunteering general," [17] said he. With relief, Washington named Lafayette for the post.

The delighted young Frenchman, at the head of nearly six thousand troops, set off after the retreating

British column, now reported to be in the vicinity of Monmouth Courthouse in New Jersey. His orders were to scout for information, place his units, and make the first strike while Washington brought up the remainder of the army for reinforcement.

Unhappily, Lafayette had only begun to carry out his orders, when late in the day, Lee rode up to supersede him in command. (Had the general changed his mind about the importance of the affair, or was it the opportunity for treachery that set him on the road? Later, it was learned that during his stay in Philadelphia, he had advised Howe on various means of destroying the American army.)

Lee was settled in a tent when Washington came up to inspect the positions. "Attack at dawn," said the Commander in Chief. After he had gone, Lafayette asked for orders. So, too, did Wayne and other unit commanders. There were none. "Not enough information yet," Charles Lee declared, and went to bed. At midnight, Washington, fearful that his prey might escape in the darkness, sent a message: *Make contact with the enemy.* Lee dispatched a small force of militia, and again turned in. There were no orders for the perplexed officers who were to launch an attack in a few hours.

Dawn came, and the general still kept his tent. Lafayette finally aroused him when a courier from Washington raced up with an order that could not be ignored: *Attack at once!* Without planning, scarcely awake, Lee sent his force into action, and the British rear turned to meet the blow.

There were no American lines of communication, no way of knowing which regiments and brigades were holding, which advancing, which falling back. Some did well, forging ahead, while others nearby faltered for want of reinforcements. The order of the day along the ragged line was confusion, and Clinton, who had sought only to escape, quickly realized that chance might have forced upon him the decisive battle of the war. He ordered up all available troops, and the British began to hit hard, thrusting the Americans back.

" Order a general advance, sir," Lafayette implored Lee.

" Sir, you don't know British soldiers. We can't stand against them," [18] Lee shouted, and called for retreat.

Many of von Steuben's pupils fell back in order, but some broke ranks and simply ran. Officers saw their units disintegrate, turning orderly retreat into a rout. They knew that a disaster was in the making, and were sure that it was at hand when a cloud of dust appeared on the road to the rear. The dire predictions of the council table were reality! The enemy had succeeded in turning their flank. They were surrounded!

Then a cheer sounded distantly. Feeble at first, it grew in volume. Someone shouted, " It's the general! " and the cry went through the horde of demoralized men who had been about to throw down their arms. They stopped in their tracks.

Lafayette never forgot the scene of Washington's arrival on the battlefield at Monmouth Courthouse. Magnificent on a great white horse, he " rode all along the lines amid the shouts of the soldiers, cheering them by his voice and example, and restoring to our standards the fortunes of the fight. I thought then, as

now, that never had I beheld so superb a man," [19] said
the Frenchman.

Others of Lee's disgusted officers saw Washington
meet Lee on the road. The Commander in Chief's
usual steely composure had cracked, and the air rang
with his rage, " till the leaves shook on the trees," [20]
said one onlooker. " Damned poltroon! " was the least
thing that Washington called his second in command
as he sent him off the field under arrest.

Wayne's men held a line while Washington set
about re-forming the troops, and after that the Americans were immovable. Clinton hurled attack after attack at their lines, and at last drew back. The exhausted Americans dropped where they stood, and
dusk had come before a counterattack could be organized. The British slipped away in the night.

Lee's cowardice, treachery, or bad judgment had
made the Battle of Monmouth Courthouse, which
should have been a blazing American victory, no better than a draw. Lieutenant Colonel Aaron Burr, as
courageous and aggressive as ever in leading his Malcolms that day, should have been among the first to
condemn such conduct. He did not. Instead, after a
court-martial had found Lee guilty of disobedience to
orders and shameful retreat, Burr offered sympathy for
the injustice done him. By this time, Burr disliked
Washington so heartily that he seemed disposed to
fellowship with anyone who had incurred the general's
wrath.

Monmouth was the last major engagement of the
war in the north. In the following year, 1779, the
British, now fighting both France and Spain as well as

rebellious colonists, turned their attention to the south. Creeping up from a first toehold in Savannah, they held Georgia and the Carolinas firmly in their grip by the end of 1780. But when Lord Cornwallis sought to add Virginia to his conquests in 1781, he allowed himself to be trapped at Yorktown by a Franco-American force and a French fleet under Admiral de Grasse.

After Cornwallis' surrender, October 19, 1781, Great Britain had had enough. However, peace negotiations, begun in 1782, dragged on for most of the year, while skirmishing continued. The preliminary treaty was signed in November, and Congress finally declared hostilities at an end on April 19, 1783, eight years and one day after the first shots on Lexington green.

CHAPTER 5

AARON BURR
"COMMENCES POLITICIAN"

AARON BURR PLAYED NO PART in the major engagements of the last years of the Revolution. Exhaustion and the terrible heat of the June day on which the Battle of Monmouth Courthouse was fought had broken his health, and early in the next year he was obliged to retire from the army. Despondent and almost penniless because of his generosity to comrades-in-arms, he did nothing for a year and a half. William Paterson, now on the New Jersey bench, heard from him. Burr wrote that he was envious of his friend's life, *serene, rural, and sentimental,* and added, I *see no company, partake of no amusements and am always grave.*[21]

He was anxious to resume his legal studies and could not force himself to make the effort. A friend who had also resigned from military service urged that they begin together. *I am confident I should acquire as much knowledge in three years with you as in six years without you,* Colonel Troup wrote, signing himself *Your unalterable friend.*[22] Robert Troup was to write repeatedly, pressing the advantages of their living and studying together.

The arrangement was never made. Perhaps Burr had been as much alarmed by the mention of a three-year period as by his friend's continual pleas for loans, for when he began reading law in Judge Paterson's office in the fall of 1780, he was suddenly in a great hurry.

Paterson had already guessed a part of the reason for this impatience to get on with a professional education. *I congratulate you on your return to civilian life, for which (I cannot forbear the thought) we must thank a certain lady not far from Paramus,*[23] he had written, upon hearing of Burr's resignation.

The lady was Mrs. Theodosia Prevost whom Burr had met when the Malcolms were stationed near her home in New Jersey. She was as unlikely a person for the handsome young colonel to fall in love with as can be imagined. Ten years his senior, she was no beauty, and she was married, the mother of five children. But she was a charming woman of culture and refinement, and Burr was fascinated by qualities that had been entirely lacking in the lovely young ladies of his acquaintance.

The affair, hopeless and unsuitable, was as much responsible for his depression during the period of idleness as was illness. He recovered both health and spirit abruptly when Mrs. Prevost, whose husband had died in the interval, accepted his proposal of marriage. Burr must have the means of earning a living before he married, however, and he lost no time in applying to William Paterson for instruction in the law.

Judge Paterson was a bit dismayed by his student. In vain he counseled a thorough grounding in the

fundamentals of the law before learning rules of practice. Burr would have nothing to do with so deliberate
an approach to the profession. He saw additional need
for haste in the changing affairs of the nation. The
war, now being fought in the southern colonies, must
surely be drawing to a close. Already there was talk
of denying to New York's Tory attorneys the right to
practice. Burr was sure that he must be ready to profit
by the situation. If a man were sharp enough, he
thought, a few months of cramming ought to enable
him to practice in satisfactory style.

So he said, in a letter to Lawyer Thomas Smith of
Haverstraw, New York, and Smith agreed. Burr
promptly left Paterson and began to study in Haverstraw, working sixteen to twenty hours a day. Six
months later, while his former comrades were prepar-
ing to hurl themselves upon Lord Cornwallis' army at
Yorktown, Colonel Burr presented himself before the
New York Supreme Court at Albany as a candidate for
the bar.

New York required three years of study for admission, and Burr, foreseeing opposition on that score,
had come prepared with a glib argument for waiving
the rule in his favor. His legal education had begun
before the Revolution, when there was no such re-
quirement, he declared, and he counted upon the jus-
tices' fairness to see that adherence to it in this case
could not fail to injure " one whose only misfortune is
having sacrificed his time, his constitution, and his
fortune, to his country." [24]

Burr cooled his heels for some time before the Court
decreed that if he could prove his qualifications to a
board of examiners, the rule might be ignored. The

board, a group of local attorneys who resented the
bumptious young man with his short-order education,
thought to humble him, but Burr survived the inquisi-
tion brilliantly. Early in 1782, he was licensed to practice law and hastened to hang out his shingle in Albany.

Clients were not slow in coming to the office of a
man with a famous family name and a record of distinguished military service. Within a few months,
Burr had all the business he could handle and decided
that he could marry. Nevertheless, he was still tread-
ing thin ice, financially. Theodosia said, in describing
their wedding, " The parson's fee took the only half
joe [a gold Portuguese coin worth about four dollars]
Burr was master of." And reporting on her new home,
" roomy but convenient," she admitted, " The want of
money is the only grievance we have." [25]

Apart from that troublesome shortage, the household was happy. Theodosia was busy with the care of
a husband and two young sons (there is no further
information concerning her daughters), and Burr, delighted with his adopted family, devoted much of his
leisure time to the supervision of the boys' education.

Contented at home and increasingly successful in
his profession, he was, nonetheless, uncertain about
the wisdom of remaining in Albany. Terms of the
peace with Great Britain were being arranged. Shortly,
British troops would evacuate New York City, and it
was there that a young attorney with brains and spirit
might expect to make his fortune. Others of Albany's
legal fraternity thought so too. Burr's friend, Robert
Troup, would soon go to the city, and Alexander Hamilton, with whom Troup had made the living-study

arrangement first proposed to Burr, was planning to quit the state capital. Burr decided to join the exodus in the fall of 1783.

The city to which he brought his family, now increased to five with the birth of daughter Theodosia, was a tiny place of scarcely twenty thousand inhabitants. A man might walk its length and breadth in an afternoon, as did John Adams, dodging livestock in dirty, narrow streets while he noted war's ravages in fire-blackened buildings, ruined wharves, and dwellings shabby with neglect.

After the peace, New York's recovery was swift, however, and again, upon opening an office, Burr saw no lack of clients. Often their business involved large sums of money, with correspondingly large fees, and he should have prospered. Actually, money was going through his hands faster than he earned it. He was perpetually in debt. His name was prominent among those of men eligible for public office, but at the moment, Aaron Burr's ambition encompassed nothing beyond the things that financial success would bring — a fine home, books, art, distinguished friends and social position. The time when personal power would be attractive was still a little way in the future.

Although he had virtually no interest in public affairs, he consented to run for the state legislature in 1784 and was elected. His attendance at the sessions was perfunctory, and when the term was up, he retired without regret. Politically indifferent for a number of years, he found home, family, and a growing practice fully absorbing.

During this period in which the liberated colonies were emerging from the exhaustion of years of war, many of Burr's friends and colleagues were passionately interested in developing a form of government that would result in a stable, prosperous nation. There was dapper little Alexander Hamilton, for instance. Frequently Burr's opponent in the courts, and occasionally his guest, Hamilton was dedicated to the idea that the Republic could survive only under a strong, centralized government, and arguing for it, had made himself a nationally recognized figure in the Philadelphia Convention of 1787 which drafted the Constitution.

Burr watched the growing importance of the small man with a speculative eye, for he began to see clear portents that politics would provide a stage on which he, too, might assume a starring role. Parties were forming as a result of the wrangling over the Convention's work, those men in favor of adopting the Constitution, led by Alexander Hamilton, calling themselves Federalists, while those who opposed it were known as anti-Federalists. Burr decided that a clever man might find advantage in avoiding firm attachment to either faction.

In 1789, the year of the Constitution's adoption and George Washington's first inauguration as President, Aaron Burr, no longer reluctant to accept public office, was named New York's Attorney General. At some time during the next year and a half he made up his mind to "commence politician," as Theodosia put it in one of her letters. With the decision, he set foot on a tragic path. Thenceforth he would spare no effort and scorn few means to achieve the power that he coveted.

The opportunity to "commence" was not long de-

layed. Early in 1791, Burr became United States Senator from New York by means of some maneuvering as
adroit and surprising as any in his later career. At that
time, the state legislatures chose the two senators, and
when Federalist Philip Schuyler's two-year term
ended, his son-in-law, Alexander Hamilton, confident
of his party's power at Albany, saw nothing in the way
of Schuyler's reelection. Assurance gave way to astonished fury when Schuyler's name was rejected for that
of Aaron Burr. The powerful Livingston family,
piqued by Federalist neglect, had joined the anti-Federalists to elect a moderate man with no strong party
ties.

There is no evidence that Burr had anything to do
with the scheme that unseated Schuyler. Perhaps he
only waited complacently for the thing to develop for
his benefit, but Hamilton did not think so. That election day at Albany marked the beginning of the bitter
enmity which ended thirteen years later with pistol fire
on a New Jersey riverbank.

CHAPTER 6

THE "WIDE WORLD" AT LAST

SENATOR AARON BURR JOURNEYED SOUTH to Philadelphia for his first session in Congress over a road that brought memories with every mile. Fourteen years earlier, in the bitter winter of 1776–1777, when the nation's fortunes and his own had been so low, he had ridden it often through Princeton and Trenton to a crossing of the Delaware. Now the countryside bore scarcely a sign of the armies that had marched and countermarched over it, and he was no longer a youngster, but a man, secure in his self-pride, about to join the councils of those who governed the United States.

Most of the fine things to which he had aspired as a young lawyer had been attained by 1791, and it pleased Burr, on this fall journey, to know that none of the men with whom he would associate in the new capital boasted a finer home, or one more elegantly furnished than Richmond Hill, which he had recently purchased. The fact that the place and its contents were mortgaged for every dollar that he could raise did not disturb his satisfaction in thinking of it.

The mansion had been occupied by Vice-President John Adams when the nation's capital was New York, and it was said that Abigail Adams had mourned for its beauties when she was obliged to move to Philadelphia. Burr was in no mood to waste sympathy on Abigail — her misfortune had been a piece of good fortune for him, one of the many that he had known since he had last seen these towns and villages.

Truly now, the " wide world " of which he had spoken so long ago was opening before him, both in Philadelphia and at Richmond Hill. He might go anywhere, be anything he chose. He had only to be careful in building relationships that might be helpful, guarded in his dealings with those men who might oppose him.

Hamilton would be one of the latter, Burr thought wryly, and knew that the Secretary of Treasury was close to another who had never shown him friendship — President George Washington.

Burr had not long been one of the distinguished company which met in the crimson-hung elegance of Congress Hall's Senate chamber before it was made clear that Washington's feelings toward him had not changed. A few weeks after his arrival, the Cabinet buzzed with rumors that the doors of the State Department were being opened at five o'clock in the morning for the senator from New York, who had no business there. Hamilton took the story to the President, and Secretary of State Thomas Jefferson, who had granted permission for the Burr researches into foreign affairs, was ordered to " get that fellow out of there."

Later, when a Senate committee proposed Burr as minister to France, Washington spoke out on the subject of his former aide: He had made it a rule of life, said the President, " never to recommend or nominate any person for a high and responsible situation in whose integrity he had not confidence." [26] Wanting confidence in Colonel Burr, he could not nominate him. " I will nominate you, Mr. Madison, or you, Mr. Monroe." [27]

Burr bore these cuts with unruffled composure. Such treatment was no more than he had expected, and it could not stand in the way of his winning a prize that he had decided he must have — a leading role in the affairs of the Republican (formerly anti-Federalist) Party. Thomas Jefferson, the party head, watched Burr's performance in the Senate uneasily, hearing at the same time of a potent political organization which the colonel was building in New York City.

The city was the key to control of New York State, and if the Republicans were ever to win a national election, they must have the state. However dangerous a rival Aaron Burr might prove to be, Jefferson needed his support.

There were others in the party, too, who saw menace in Burr's growing importance. An unidentified Virginian expressed their thoughts: *I have watched the movements of Mr. Burr with attention, and have discovered traits of character which sooner or later will give us much trouble. He has an unequalled talent for attaching men to his views, and forming combinations of which he is always the center. He is determined to play a first part.*[28]

The Virginian had judged his man well. A year after Burr's entry into the Senate, he had gained sufficient stature among his fellows to be mentioned as candidate for the Vice-Presidency, and in spite of withdraw-

ing his name, received one electoral vote for the office.
Four years later, when the Federalists were again victorious, electing John Adams to the Presidency, he gar-
nered thirty votes. For a man who had interested himself in politics only eight years before, Burr had come
a long way.

In the letters written from Philadelphia at this period to the two Theodosias, he revealed the best side of
his nature with his concern for their welfare. During
the first years in the Senate, his wife's failing health
was the subject of deep anxiety. He consulted doctors
in Philadelphia, sent their recommendations, and when
she was no longer able to write, begged his ten-year-
old daughter for news of her. After Mrs. Burr's death
in 1794, lovely little Theodosia, for whom he was as
ambitious as for himself, became the most important
person in his life.

Long before, Burr had promised himself that his
daughter's training would prove what few people then
believed — that a well-educated woman could be the
charming equal of any man. Her schooling had begun,
under his direction, when she was little more than a
baby. At the age of three, she wrote him her first letter, and in her tenth year, she was reading Latin and
French.

Delighted with the child, as he was always to be,
Burr wrote of the difficulty he had had in finding a gift
for *an intelligent, well-informed girl of nine years old.
I found plenty of fairy tales and such nonsense, fit for
the generality of children of nine or ten years old,*[29] but
nothing would do until he found *a handsomely bound
work of fancy, replete with instruction and amusement.*

He insisted that she write him frequently when he

was absent, and Theodosia knew that she must take great care with the letters, for her father wanted to show them off to his Senate colleagues. Often she disappointed him, and he scolded her about errors. *That word "recieved" still escapes your attention. Try again. The words "wold" and "shold" are mere carelessness. . . . Learn the difference between "then" and "than."* [30] Badly constructed sentences drew his ire too. On one occasion, after chiding her about such a sentence, he added, *By-the-by, I took the liberty to erase the redundant "it" before I showed the letter.* [31]

(The confession that he had altered his child's letter, in order to boast about it, reveals Aaron Burr as clearly as anything he ever did or said. Consuming pride and a talent for deceit, the characteristics that were to wreck his life, led him to make that careful erasure.)

Theodosia was fourteen years old when her father's term as senator ended. Since her mother's death three years before, she had been the mistress of Richmond Hill, presiding over the parties her father loved to give with a mature charm that astonished his guests.

Burr was never happier than as the radiant host at such affairs, but upon his return from the last session in Philadelphia, it seemed that they must end — at least, for a time. His financial position, always precarious, was now desperate. Extravagant in his tastes, he had borrowed recklessly in order to live as he thought he must, and when notes that he could not hope to pay fell due, he borrowed again to satisfy them. In the years since the move from Albany, he had built a mountain of indebtedness which at last threatened to topple upon him. Creditors were at his heels continually, and in his urgent need for cash, Burr sold the furnishings of Richmond Hill. All the fine furniture, carpets, mirrors, and objects of art for which he had paid a fortune went for $3,500 to pay only one of his debts.

Hamilton and his Federalist friends knew of Burr's embarrassment, and they talked gleefully of political ruin for him too. Since they were now in control of the state legislature, Philip Schuyler would be sent to Philadelphia to take the Senate seat of which he had been deprived, and Burr must go back to his law office. He was no longer a threat.

His enemies underestimated Burr. In the stripped and echoing rooms at Richmond Hill, he was already planning the next moves to bend fortune to his will. So the Senate was a thing of the past, he told the young men who formed the core of his support in New York City. There were things that one could do at a lower level that might yield more profit in the long run. For instance, he could run for the state Assembly — they would see what could be accomplished there, he promised.

He made good his bid for the Assembly in 1797, and during the next two years, his activities in Albany did little to quiet the whispers about Colonel Burr's gift for intriguing on his own behalf. For a first thing, he interested himself in liberalizing the laws covering bankruptcy — surely a change that would be of personal benefit, said his enemies. Indeed, Colonel Troup, the "unalterable friend" of his youth, who had altered considerably, thought it perhaps the only reason he had sought so humble an office.

Then there was the Holland Land Company affair. In his efforts to gain fortune quickly, Burr had involved himself deeply with this Dutch company which was speculating in American public lands, and when a bill to benefit the company by permitting aliens to hold New York State land came before the legislature, he agreed to sponsor it.

That would have been enough to set opposition tongues to wagging, but after the measure had passed, rumors of bribery fueled the fire of Federalist indignation. Several of the legislators had been handed substantial amounts of money, it was said, and among them was Aaron Burr. (The records of the company leave no doubt that the assertion was true, but Burr always insisted that the $5,500 written after his name was a loan.)

What sort of trickery might be expected next from this man? the Federalists wondered. Would he try to mend his political as well as his personal fortunes in the Assembly? Watching him with increased vigilance, they found nothing suspicious. In fact, much that he did seemed to be truly in the public interest. During the period of the quasi-war with France, he allied himself with the opposition in his concern for New York City's defenses, and it was thought that he could only have the welfare of its people in mind with his proposal for the incorporation of a company to provide pure water.

Most of the Federalists did not hesitate to join their opponents in support of a measure to do away with the contaminated water that had cost thousands of lives in recurring epidemics of yellow fever. The joker in the bill, lost in the fine print, was revealed to them only after its passage — the Manhattan Company might use surplus capital in any way it wished.

Investors poured money into the venture, and shortly Burr was able to realize the primary objective of the water company bill. He opened a bank, the city's first under Republican control.

Hamilton was livid with rage. Heretofore, he had had the credit of the Bank of New York and the Bank of the United States under his personal thumb, and the businessman who needed a loan must show his willingness to vote the Federalist ticket. If he did not, he was simply wasting his time. It may be imagined that many a man who might have been a Republican persuaded himself to a more profitable allegiance before entering a New York bank.

Again and again, Federalists in Albany had defeated Republican efforts to charter a third bank, but now Burr had broken their stranglehold on New York finance. He had tricked the legislature into sanctioning the Bank of the Manhattan Company (still in existence as the Chase Manhattan Bank) which, in the following year, was to play a large part in electing a president of the United States.

CHAPTER 7

THOMAS JEFFERSON'S
VICE-PRESIDENT

FOR A LONG TIME PAST, Burr had had his eyes fixed on the election of 1800, when President John Adams would be running for a second term against Thomas Jefferson. A mighty prize would be at stake at the polls that year, for if Jefferson were victorious, what was more logical than to suppose that his running mate would be his successor in the course of time? Aaron Burr intended to be that man. President of the United States by 1808, at the latest! — that was his dream, and only a few obstacles lay in the way of its realization.

The first was the necessity of carrying a key election in New York State in the spring of the year. At that time only five states gave men any semblance of chance to vote directly in a national election. In the other eleven, including New York, the legislatures chose presidential electors from the party in power. Albany's electors would cast important ballots in November, for with the agrarian South favoring Jefferson, and New England solidly behind Adams, New York would probably decide the election. It had been agreed in Republican councils that Burr would be the vice-presidential nominee if he could carry his state for the party.

Federalists had been in the majority at Albany in 1799. Burr knew that a substantial number of them must be unseated in 1800 if the state were to go for Jefferson. The prospects were not bright. New York, like most of the other states, required that a man must own property in order to have a voice in government. As a result, only a few more than twelve thousand men, of a total population of more than three hundred thousand, were qualified to vote. A large part of that elite group, naturally inclined toward conservative Federalist policies, lived in New York City, and it was there that Burr set out to win the election.

Equally astute in political matters, Thomas Jefferson saw the importance of the city too. *In New-York all depends on the success of the city election,*[32] he wrote to James Madison, and he was speaking of the national results when he continued, *We may say, that if . . . [it] is in favour of the republican ticket, the issue will be republican.*[33] Jefferson might have some doubts about Colonel Burr, but he certainly wished him well in his efforts that spring.

Aaron Burr was then in his forty-fifth year. The dark head was balding, the features were sharper than they had been in his handsome youth, but the snapping black eyes spoke of a mind more agile than ever, and he was still charming. The " talent of attaching men to his views," particularly young ones, was unimpaired. Years later, Matthew L. Davis described Burr's youthful supporters (including himself) as *friends of the most ardent and devoted kind . . . of gallant bearing and disinterested views.*[34] Confident of their man's patriotism and judgment, and *feeling that he was inca-pable of deceiving them, they seemed willing . . . to hazard their lives and fortunes in his support,*[35] accord-ing to Davis.

Some of the young men had long been engaged on a project that had puzzled many of Burr's opponents. " Why is the colonel so interested in the Society of St. Tammany? " they asked each other. He had not joined the society himself — such a company of mechanics and laborers would be much too lowly for his tastes, but a number of his friends had. It was known that William Van Ness, Matthew Davis, and John Swart-wout, among others, had been busy converting what had been a social organization into a sort of Burr Ad-miration Society. It was loyal and vocal support, the Federalists admitted, but most Tammanyites were landless and could not vote. In what possible way could the society serve the colonel? they wondered.

Convinced that it was a political weapon, they un-derstood it no better than they did some others that were forged at Richmond Hill and in the Burr town house during the winter and early spring of 1800. Un-der Burr's direction, his aides worked endlessly at the task of mounting the first modern political campaign. The city must be charted and every voter listed, with the names of those able to contribute funds under-scored. Burr sent some of his lieutenants out canvass-ing door-to-door and named others to conduct delicate interviews where much more than money was at stake.

The latter young men were aghast when they learned what was expected of them. " Ask ex-Governor Clinton to run for the state legislature! " they pro-tested. " The old man is no friend of yours, and why should he want to run for a legislator's seat, in any case? Brockholst Livingston? The same thing with him. And old General Horatio Gates? — a national hero, not a politician. He will never consent."

Burr was firm with them. " The party must have the most powerful slate of candidates possible — twelve names so distinguished that the voter who isn't committed to either party will have no doubt about casting his ballot for them. Your job is to get these men to agree to run."

Davis remembered that the task was not easy. No one expected a Republican victory, and Burr's chosen nominees *shrank from being set up as targets to be shot at.*[36] After a great deal of persuasion, nine of them agreed reluctantly, but Clinton, Gates, and Livingston were adamant in their refusals.

Burr added his pleas to those already made, and at last, Livingston consented to run if Clinton and Gates would. Gates said it depended on what Clinton did, and Clinton, liking nothing about the situation but the possibility of beating Hamilton and his party, agreed to be drafted.

Everyone concerned in the matter was warned to keep his mouth closed on the subject of the Republican nominees. " The time to show this ticket," said Burr, " is after Hamilton has announced the Federalist slate. I have been informed that it will be a group of nobodies."

Shortly, a Burr spy in the Federalist ranks produced the list. Hamilton, confident of victory, had named friends upon whom he could depend to carry out a pet project of his own — the ouster of President John Adams in favor of Charles C. Pinckney of South Carolina.

" Now, I have him all hollow! " [37] Burr is reported to have said upon examining the list.

The Federalists were stunned when names of the opposing candidates were at last revealed. It was too late to make changes in their own slate, and none realized better than Alexander Hamilton the significance of what Burr had accomplished. He knew that victory could no longer be counted on as a certainty, that he must be ready to put forth such effort as he never had before.

When the polls opened in New York City on April 29 for the three-day election, Hamilton mounted his white horse to ride furiously from one ward to another, exhorting voters to stand by the party that favored their interests as propertied men. More than a few sly grins greeted his pleas, for there were men in the waiting groups whose credentials to vote were scarcely dry.

Good Tammanyites all, they had marched to the polls, claiming the right to cast a ballot by reason of part ownership of property. " A twentieth interest in a plot of land? A thirtieth? " officials had queried. " No matter," replied the counselors who were guiding formerly landless men through the intricacies that led to the ballot box. " New York law says that all owners in a joint tenancy are qualified to vote."

" Fraud! " the Federalists cried when the trick was exposed. But there was no fraud about it. Burr had made sure of the law, and his Bank of the Manhattan Company had loaned much of the money that created scores of new voters.

The party machinery was in full swing during the balloting, Burr sparing himself no more than he did his lieutenants. On the last day, Davis snatched time to report to Albert Gallatin: *This day he [Burr] has remained at the polls of the Seventh Ward ten hours without intermission. Pardon this hasty scrawl. I have not ate for fifteen hours.*[38]

The election ended with the setting of the sun on May 1, and the nation's Republicans awaited the results eagerly. A few hours later, the tally was far enough advanced to show a Burr victory. The man who had made himself the first American political boss had ensured that his state's votes for the next President of the United States would be Republican.

A few days later, party leaders, meeting in Philadelphia, named their candidates — Thomas Jefferson and Aaron Burr.

Hamilton was more than alarmed — he was wild. The intemperance of his words is a clear indication of his state of mind: Jefferson was an " atheist in religion and fanatic in politics," [39] while Burr, " as unprincipled and dangerous a man as any country can hold," [40] was even then "intriguing with all his might" to overthrow his running mate. Jefferson was only slightly less to be feared than Burr, cried Hamilton, for the man who had written in the Declaration of Independence, *All men are created equal,* intended to turn the country over to the masses, and it should be evident to anyone with sense that none but men of wealth, education, and position were qualified to have a voice in public affairs. Hamilton sincerely believed this.

In the months after the New York election, while other states were still balloting, the Federalists followed Hamilton's lead in campaigning. The Republicans concentrated their attack on the Adams administration's Alien and Sedition Acts which plainly nullified the constitutional rights of free speech and a free press. According to the provisions of these measures, a citizen who criticized the Government (that is, any elected official) was guilty of a crime; the alien who did so would be deported.

The height of feeling aroused during the campaign of 1800 had not been matched in any of the three previous national elections, and it did not die away when the final results were made known with the announcement of South Carolina's electoral votes in December. The country had gone Republican, but it had not elected a President. At that time, the Constitution provided for each elector to cast two votes. The Presidency went to the nominee with the highest number, the Vice-Presidency to the next man, regardless of party. The tally of votes in 1800 — Jefferson seventy-three, Burr seventy-three, Adams sixty-five, Pinckney sixty-four, Jay one — had thrown the election into the House of Representatives, which would decide upon a President in February. The fight was on again.

Jefferson was taken aback by the tie vote. He had not doubted, he wrote Burr, that arrangements had been made to shift a few votes, so that it could not have occurred. In reply, Burr was comforting: Jefferson must not worry, he said. *My personal friends are perfectly informed of my wishes on the subject and can never think of diverting a single vote from you.*[41] A week earlier, he had indeed written a letter, stating this position: *Every man who knows me ought to know that I would utterly disclaim all competition. Friends would dishonour my views and insult my feelings by any such suspicion.*[42]

Perhaps Burr was sincere when he wrote the words; perhaps he was not, and only intended them for the record. At any rate, he did not repeat himself during the next seven weeks of exciting rumors that the Federalists in the House might make him President, rather than Jefferson.

The opposition move to elect Burr had started almost as soon as it was known that the Republicans had been victorious. It was " the opinion, not of light and fanciful, but of serious and considerable men, that Burr must be preferred to Jefferson," [43] according to one Federalist. These men were not slow in approaching Burr. *Take no step whatever by which the choice of the House can be impeded or embarrassed. Keep the game perfectly in your own hands, but do not answer this letter,* [44] he was advised by one of the leaders in the plot.

Hamilton, at first unbelieving, fought the growing sentiment for Burr with words of horror: " He is bankrupt beyond redemption, except by the plunder of his country. . . . If he can, he will certainly disturb our institutions, to secure to himself *permanent power,* and with it *wealth.*" [45] But Hamilton was no longer a leader of influence among the Federalists. They feared Jefferson, who was " deeply imbued with false principles of government," more than they believed in the monstrous scoundrel of Hamilton's picture.

A Connecticut Federalist asserted mildly that Burr held " no pernicious theories." Like most of his fellows from that part of the country, he favored Burr's election, seeing it as a means of escaping a government dominated by radical southerners. In the north, there was even a bit of muttering about secession, if Jefferson became President.

With the beginning of the year 1801, the war of words grew more heated, and it was suspected that Burr was playing an active part in it. The letter disclaiming all competition could have been " intended as a cover to blind his own party," said one of Hamilton's friends, adding that he had talked with Republicans close to Burr who " distinctly stated that he is willing to consider the Federalists as his friends, and to accept the office of President as their gift. I take it for granted that Mr. Burr would not only gladly accept the office, but will neglect no means in his power to secure it." [46] The Governor of South Carolina said he had been assured " by a gentleman who lately had some conversation with Mr. B. on this subject that he is disposed to maintain and expand our systems."

Jefferson noted all such reports with narrowed eyes. Outright enmity was replacing the earlier distrust, for he did not doubt now that Burr was willing to usurp the presidential chair. If it were not so, he had only to publish, for all the world to see, his refusal to accept the Federalist's efforts on his behalf. Instead, he was playing a silent game hundreds of miles distant from Washington, the raw, new capital where the election tie would be resolved.

Undoubtedly, Burr had powerful friends at work there, and it may have been a part of his strategy to remain at home, but there was another reason too. Nine days before the House met for the crucial ballot, eighteen-year-old Theodosia was married to Joseph Alston of South Carolina. Watching the beloved child depart for a new home, Burr remembered the family of which he had been so proud as a young man. It had melted away at last, leaving him quite alone. Fortunately, the first days of loneliness gave promise of being the most important of his life, and he sought consolation in thinking of the exciting conferences that must, even then, be taking place in Washington.

He may have wrinkled a fastidious nose at the thought of living there, for in 1801, the capital boasted little more than an unfinished capitol building, scarcely fit for occupancy, the President's house, a muddy mile distant, and a boardinghouse or two whose accommodations compared most unfavorably with the fine hostelries of Philadelphia and New York. The government was, in fact, being conducted by men who were enduring the discomforts of pioneers.

The winter of 1800–1801 had been raw and chill, and on the morning of February 11, when the House met to elect a President, snow, borne on a bitter wind, was falling. Congressmen shuddered with cold in their drafty chamber and were concerned that one of their number, Joseph Nicholson of Maryland, had been carried from a sickbed to cast his vote.

The first ballot was taken in early afternoon — fifty-five votes for Burr, fifty-one for Thomas Jefferson. Burr would have been President if a majority of individuals had been sufficient, but according to the Constitution, the voting was by states, with a majority of nine required to elect. Eight states had gone to Jefferson and six to Burr. Again the vote was taken, with the same result, and again and again. Thirty-five times in the next six days the count revealed that not a man had stirred from his initial commitment.

It had been clear from the beginning that the shift of only a few votes within the delegations would end the contest, and finally the Burr supporters began to give way, fearing that the Government might be destroyed if the deadlock were not broken. The thirty-sixth ballot, taken on February 17, elected Thomas Jefferson President of the United States, and the exhausted congressmen called for adjournment, determined to make another such election impossible. (The Twelfth Amendment to the Constitution, passed in 1804, provided for separate ballots for President and Vice-President.)

The new Vice-President professed himself pleased with the result. He had never hinted (on paper, at least) that any other outcome would be desirable, and he took up his duties as President of the Senate with a dignified competence that won applause from many of the senators.

During the next two years, however, it gradually became apparent that the contested election had been a disastrous affair for Burr. Thomas Jefferson, now allied with the Clinton and Livingston factions of New York's Republicans, was doing everything in his power to break his late rival politically. There would be no second term for Aaron Burr.

No matter how dark the future might promise to be, Burr always had the ability to see it in a favorable light, and this was true during his term as Vice-President. Surrounded by enemies in Washington, saying little concerning his prospects, he cast about for some way in which to use the political power of his New York organization. The opportunity was presented to him early in 1804, when it was made clear that another mild flirtation with the Federalist party might yield a prize to match the one he had lost on February 17, 1801.

The terms of the affair had been intimated to Burr at a dinner attended by a number of senators from New England. The Vice-President must know, said the senators, that their states were restless. The Virginians were in complete control of the National Government and, with the Louisiana Territory (acquired in 1803) under their domination, were likely to remain so. New England considered itself a part of a loose confederation of states and had the right to separate whenever it chose, the senators continued. The time to do so was now. It was to be hoped that New York, New Jersey, and eastern Pennsylvania would join the exodus. New York was of prime importance, of course. "And she will come along if we can elect a governor who will support us," said the senators.

Burr had no difficulty in reading the message: "We Federalists will support your candidacy for governor if you will give us your aid in dissolving the Union." Moreover, there were broad hints, in the long conferences that followed, that no better head of the newly created nation could be found than the governor of its most important state, New York. Again, the little man rehearsed in private for a coveted role.

With no hope of gaining his own party's nomination for any sort of office, Burr filed as an independent, the Republicans naming Morgan Lewis as their candidate.

The Vice-President began his campaign confident of success. The promised Federalist support throughout the state, added to the majority that he could count upon in New York City, would doubtless produce a victory. Hamilton would be heard from, of course, but it was common knowledge in the Burr camp that he no longer commanded much attention from his party. Spirits were high at Richmond Hill during the spring of 1804.

As he was expected to do, Alexander Hamilton threw himself, with all the vigor at his command, into a fight from which he had nothing to gain or lose personally. Inking his pen for words as furious as any he had ever used in describing Burr, he was certain that, this time, he was battling for the very existence of the United States of America. Unfortunately, some of his extravagant language found its way into print.

Venomous as Hamilton's words proved to be, they were outdone by those of many of Burr's former friends in the Republican Party. In particular, Editor James Cheetham, DeWitt Clinton's employee, spared nothing in his catalogue of the Vice-President's sins. As the savage contest drew to a close, Burr supporters were reduced to indignant denials on behalf of their candidate.

The election took place in April, and early returns from the city made it appear that the forces of disunion had triumphed. Burr was the victor there. But when the results of the three-day balloting had been counted, it was apparent that Hamilton's efforts upstate had been successful. Morgan Lewis was the new governor of New York, and disunion was, for the moment, a dead issue.

Aaron Burr, in his mid-forties, at the height of his intellectual powers, had been destroyed politically. " We shall hear no more of him," said his enemies.

CHAPTER 8

THE DUEL AT WEEHAWKEN

OUTWARDLY, BURR REMAINED SERENE and cheerful in the face of his defeat for the governorship. Immediately following the final tally of votes he wrote to Theodosia: *The election is lost by a great majority. So much the better.*⁴⁷ Those whom he encountered in going about his business in the city heard much the same thing. There were none of the recriminations that might have been expected from a man who had had the last political door slammed upon him.

Alone at Richmond Hill, Burr dropped his pose, giving way to bitterness that grew like a swelling infection. That spring he had no eyes for the fresh beauty of lawns and trees or for the farther vistas of hills and river. He did not dwell upon the bare loneliness of the magnificent rooms. It was clear to him that he would not possess Richmond Hill much longer, for he was ruined financially as well as politically. The property had been mortgaged to the limit, and there was a judgment of $40,000 against him. The years of folly must be paid for at last.

There were snubs to endure too. The rich and famous, whom Burr had formerly entertained so grandly, ignored him. Jerome Bonaparte, brother of the French Emperor, who had been his friend in Washington, administered the crowning slight — he and his wife, Betsey, did not deign to call upon the Vice-President when they visited New York. Burr maintained his tone of light amusement in writing to Theodosia about these insults, but his face settled into hard lines as he named for himself those whose slanders he held to be responsible.

Months before, he had said to a friend, " I am determined to call out the first man of any respectability concerned in these publications about me." [48]

" Cheetham is the worst of the lot," the friend remarked, " but you can't duel with him — he's not a gentleman. If you want satisfaction in that direction, you must sue."

" I agree," Burr replied, " but DeWitt Clinton should be made to answer for Cheetham's vile accusations. Although there's no proof of it, I can't doubt he's Clinton's hireling."

" You will never get proof of that. Forget DeWitt Clinton." There was relief in the tone of the response, for dueling, long a means of settling quarrels between gentlemen, was now widely condemned. It was certainly not a practice in which the Vice-President of the United States should engage.

Nevertheless, Burr did not forget the threat he had voiced. Following his friend's advice, he filed suit against Cheetham, but he knew that no amount of legal satisfaction would cancel the memory of the journalist's sneers and slanderous fabrications. On one occasion Cheetham had especially riled Burr with a hint of cowardice. *Is the Vice-President sunk so low as to submit to be insulted by General Hamilton?* [49] Cheetham had asked.

"No, by Jupiter, no!" Burr had exclaimed. "All I need is proof. When I get it, I shall act!" Hamilton was the ancient enemy. He had tried to cut Aaron Burr down at every opportunity. He was the one who ought to be called upon for satisfaction on the field of honor.

Six weeks after the election Burr had the evidence he wanted. His eyes flashed as he read a newspaper clipping that had come to his hands. In a letter written by Dr. Charles Cooper and published in Albany, there was a remark reported to have been made by Hamilton: "Mr. Burr is a dangerous man who ought not to be trusted with the reins of government." The doctor had added, *I could detail to you a still more despicable opinion which General Hamilton has expressed of Mr. Burr.* [50]

These were fighting words. On June 17, 1804, Burr sent a message to his friend, Federal Judge William Van Ness: *Will you call at Richmond Hill tomorrow morning on a matter of personal business?*

Van Ness found Burr finishing a letter to Alexander Hamilton. "If he will not apologize, I shall call him out," said Burr. "Will you act for me?"

Van Ness agreed. It is not known whether he tried to dissuade his friend at the outset of the disastrous affair, but in any event a few hours later he presented himself at Hamilton's door, murmuring about "a communication which will deserve your attention."

Hamilton must have known as he broke the seal what was impending. He may even have wondered why this visit had been so long delayed, for he knew that many of his remarks about Aaron Burr were such as might result in an affair of honor.

A copy of the Cooper letter was folded in the note. Hamilton glanced at it. Then he read Burr's words: *You must perceive, sir, the necessity of a prompt and unqualified acknowledgment or denial of the use of any expressions which would warrant the assertions of Mr. Cooper.*[51] Again Hamilton turned his attention to the letter.

At length, he said, " I do not see how the publication of such a letter can authorize Colonel Burr to call upon me in this way. The references are so general and undefined that I could not give a specific answer. If he will cite particular expressions, I will recognize or disavow them."

Van Ness was stiff and formal in his role. " The laws of honor justify the colonel in inquiring of any gentleman whether he had uttered expressions that imparted dishonor," he declared.

" I do not think you are right in your position, but I will go over this and give you an answer," Hamilton agreed reluctantly.

The message, delivered at Richmond Hill a couple of days later, was a repetition of what Van Ness had already heard: Hamilton was ready to deal with specific remarks, but not with the general implication of Cooper's letter.

" A mere evasion," Burr snapped. Again he wrote to his enemy, sneering that he had found in his words *nothing of that sincerity and delicacy which you profess to value. Your letter has furnished me with new reasons for requiring a definite reply.*[52]

" This is the sort of letter I had hoped not to receive, a rude and offensive message," Hamilton told Van

Ness, when he had read Burr's words. He declared that he would not answer it. "I shall have nothing more to say on the subject. Colonel Burr must pursue whatever course he deems proper."

"Take a little time to deliberate," Van Ness advised.

"No, you have my answer," Hamilton cried. "He must do what he thinks is proper!"

Hamilton actually signed his death warrant with these remarks. He knew that a duel was inevitable when he called upon Nathaniel Pendleton during the evening. "It appears that I shall stand in need of a friend," he said, describing the trouble with Burr. "Will you act for me?"

Pendleton was horrified and thought the matter might be patched up without dishonor to Hamilton. Four days of conferences between the seconds ensued. They were fruitless. "No denial or declaration will be satisfactory unless it be general," [53] said Van Ness and presented for Hamilton's signature an "explanation" which was, in effect, a groveling apology for all the derogatory remarks that Hamilton had ever made about his enemy. Pendleton rejected it, of course. "General Hamilton is sorry to be able to discern nothing short of predetermined hostility in the ground that Colonel Burr has assumed. He has instructed me to receive the message which you have it in charge to deliver," he told Van Ness.

On the following day, June 27, 1804, Van Ness appeared at Pendleton's door, bearing the message — an invitation from Aaron Burr to Alexander Hamilton to meet for the purpose of a "private interview."

The two seconds came to agreement on plans for the duel several days later: The time, an early morning hour of July 11; the place, a well-known dueling ground on the New Jersey shore of the Hudson River; the weapons, pistols at ten paces.

The secret of an impending duel between two of the nation's most important men was well-kept. Not more than a dozen people — principals, seconds, surgeon, and boatmen — knew what was afoot. Friends and associates of Burr and Hamilton remarked later that nothing in the conduct of either man during the long period between June 18 and July 11 had revealed that their enmity was about to be resolved.

Quiet and reserved as always, Burr was much alone at Richmond Hill during those days. However, on Theodosia's birthday, June 23, he invited a group of friends to dine and described the party for her: *I had your picture brought to table and put it in your place. . . . We laughed an hour and danced an hour and drank your health.*

Still, he must have had moments of trepidation, perhaps even of remorse over the action that he had taken, for a few days later, he wrote his daughter that he had been *shivering with cold all day, though in perfect health.* At sunset, he had had a fire built and had huddled close to it.

Hamilton went to court daily, arguing his cases competently, displaying to friends and clients his usual cheerfulness. Like Burr, he had little company during the weeks before the duel, his wife and seven children having moved to their country home in the woods of upper Manhattan. He joined them there as frequently as possible, betraying by no word or gesture the existence of a threat to his life.

In the company of his family, Hamilton often

thought of his son, Philip, who, had he lived, would now be twenty-two years old. Three years before, Philip had been killed in a duel. " I called that murder — a youth against an experienced duelist," the father mused, thinking of his son. " Will they also call it murder if Aaron Burr kills me? " The alternative, his opponent's death, never occurred to him, for Alexander Hamilton had no intention of firing at Burr. As a gentleman, he could not refuse a challenge — indeed, he had invited it; but he proposed to do nothing more than present himself at the dueling ground to satisfy the demands of honor.

On July 4, a week before the date set for the meeting, both men attended a festive banquet of the Society of the Cincinnati. Hamilton, president of the group, sat at a distance from Burr. They did not speak. Others of the Cincinnati remembered later that Burr had little to say and paid no attention to Hamilton until a clamor arose for " The Drum," a ballad that the general had often sung at meetings. Then he turned in his chair, leaned on the table and studied his enemy with hard-eyed attention.

Hamilton had been cheerful, even merry during the festivities, but he seemed reluctant to sing. " Not tonight," he protested.

" The Drum," " The Drum," chanted the Cincinnati and would not stop.

" Well, you shall have it," Hamilton agreed at last. One wonders if he glanced at Aaron Burr as he sang, and glanced again, seeing the stillness of the man and his unwavering, somber stare.

There was much for Hamilton to do in the next week. Other residents of New York's Cedar Street ob-

served that the windows of No. 52 glowed with can-
dlelight far into the night, and they speculated on the
nature of the business that kept their distinguished
neighbor so late at work. Surely it must be important,
they reasoned, for there had been much coming and
going at General Hamilton's. His good friend, Nathaniel Pendleton, in particular, had often been seen hur-
rying to and fro on errands.

Pendleton was still at No. 52 when most of Cedar
Street retired on the night of July 10. Hour after hour,
he had waited quietly while Hamilton continued to
work at his desk, filling pages with a clear, bold script.
" I have almost done," he told his companion at last.
" I shall not keep you much longer."

" You must not concern yourself for me," Pendleton
replied, " but you should get some rest. It is late."

" There is only another little note that I must write
to Mrs. Hamilton. Then, you may have it all — will, financial statement, trust arrangements, and letters."

Again, Hamilton turned to his desk and drew
toward him a fresh sheet of paper. In the waning hours
of July 10, he had a strong premonition of disaster, and
he wanted to make sure that his wife would under-
stand in what spirit he had set forth for the appointment with Aaron Burr. He wrote, *The scruples of a
Christian have determined me to expose my own life
to any extent rather than subject myself to the guilt
of taking the life of another. . . . God's will be done!
The will of a merciful God must be good. Once more
adieu, my darling, darling wife. AH.*⁵⁴

" There, I have finished," he said, sanding and seal-
ing the message. " In the event of my death, you will
give this to Mrs. Hamilton with the other that I wrote.

I have told her that I do not propose to be responsible for taking a life."

Pendleton was silent for a moment. He shook his head. " It will be murder. You may be sure that Colonel Burr will fire. I have reason to believe that he has been practicing with his pistols."

" That will not deter me. I have made up my mind not to fire at Colonel Burr."

" I urge you not to do this! You must defend yourself."

" My friend, it is the effect of a religious scruple, and does not admit of reasoning. It is useless to say more on the subject, as my purpose is definitely fixed."

As he left Hamilton, Pendleton thought: At first opportunity in the morning, I must let Van Ness know of this. If Burr learns of the general's resolution, the thing may yet blow over. Then, he shook his head again. It was too much to hope for.

Nevertheless, in the very early morning of July 11, Pendleton sought out Van Ness and told him of Hamilton's decision. Absolutely nothing else is known of this meeting. Van Ness never acknowledged it. Whether he told Burr that Hamilton would not fire at him is not known. If he did, Burr must truly be counted a murderer; if not, then Van Ness ought to be held accountable for Hamilton's death.

At some time during the evening of July 10, Burr, too, wrote a last letter. Addressed to Theodosia, it is far different in its tone from the one that Elizabeth Hamilton was to receive. There is a light, whimsical touch in the instructions for the disposition of his personal effects — all that he had to bequeath — and he closed the letter on a characteristic note: *With a little*

*more perseverance, determination, and industry, you
will obtain all that my ambition and vanity had fondly
imagined. . . . Adieu. Adieu. A. Burr.*[55]

That done, he threw off his outer garments and lay
down on a sofa in the library. John Swartwout, who
spent the night at Richmond Hill, found him sleeping
soundly at dawn.

Shortly after five o'clock, Burr mounted his horse
and, accompanied by Swartwout, Van Ness, who was
awkwardly managing a large umbrella, and one or
two others, he set out for the riverbank. Little was said
on the brief journey — only a word or two about the
warmth of the morning and the fact that mist lying on
the river would conceal their passage. A barge with a
pair of boatmen lay ready for them at the water's edge
and, presently, four of the party embarked for the
crossing.

Long before the time of the Burr-Hamilton duel,
gentlemen of New York who had quarrels to settle had
discovered a narrow ledge in the high rock cliffs which
border the Hudson near Weehawken, New Jersey.
This shelf, no more than four feet wide at one point
and barely long enough to allow the customary ten
paces, offered perfect seclusion for their " interviews."
Twenty feet above the river, it was inaccessible except
by water. No houses were visible, and there was no
path from above.

The ledge was on the property of an old sea captain
who disapproved violently of the use to which it had
been put. He lived at some distance from the place,
but whenever he had heard rumors of a duel and saw
barges approaching his portion of the cliff, he came
scrambling over the rocks, prepared to call a halt to the

proceedings by one means or another.

Unhappily, the old man had heard nothing of the trouble between the Vice-President and General Hamilton, and he was sleeping soundly when Aaron Burr and Van Ness mounted the rocks to the shelf. Nor did he see the barge carrying Alexander Hamilton approach a half hour later. It is said that the captain lived out his life, believing that, had he risen early on the morning of July 11, 1804, he could have raised an outcry that would have saved Hamilton's life.

Burr and his friend had found the shelf overgrown with brush, plainly long unused. They busied themselves with clearing it during the interval of waiting. When Hamilton and Pendleton appeared, there was a stiff word of greeting between the parties. The seconds conferred a moment, loaded the pistols, and stepped off ten paces. Lots were drawn — the choice of position fell to Hamilton; Pendleton was to call the fatal word, " Present."

Hamilton chose the upper end of the ledge, facing east. If he glanced away at the moment, he saw the broad reach of the river widening where it empties into New York Bay, and Staten Island, a blue outline in the distance. Across the river, the forest-fringed shore of Manhattan Island, with the little city at its tip, would have been half hidden in mist. He searched a pocket for spectacles and put them on.

Burr took his place. The seconds presented the weapons.

" Are you ready? " Pendleton asked.

" Yes," said Burr.

Hamilton had been sighting along his pistol barrel. " Yes," he said, dropping it to his side.

" Present! " Pendleton cried.

Burr's pistol cracked. Hamilton spun on his toes, his arm upraised as he fired into a tree. He began to fall. Burr sprang forward as though to aid the stricken man, and Van Ness saw on his face an expression of startled horror.

" No, no! " Van Ness cried, snapping open the umbrella and raising it over Burr. " The surgeon must not see you here. He cannot say that you were here if he has not seen you." He pulled him away toward the barge, Burr glancing back once at his fallen adversary.

Pendleton had reached Hamilton in one bound and lifted him from the ground a little. " Surgeon! " he cried desperately.

" This is a mortal wound, doctor," [56] Hamilton said and lost consciousness as Dr. David Hosack came up.

" I told the fellow, I told him this morning," Pendleton muttered in agony, as the barge carried the dying man back to Manhattan. " They are murderers."

Thirty hours later, Alexander Hamilton lost his hopeless battle for life, and Pendleton's charge rang throughout the city.

Before nightfall it was apparent that Aaron Burr had forfeited whatever chance he may have had to regain the esteem and confidence of the nation. He was never to escape the consequences of the tragic duel at Weehawken.

CHAPTER 9

JOURNEY TO THE WEST

THERE WAS AN UNEXPECTED CALLER at Richmond Hill early on the morning of July 11 — a young Burr kinsman, en route to the city, who stopped off on the chance of getting breakfast. He was cordially received by the master of the house, who promptly tendered the hoped-for invitation. The conversation at table was casual, Burr inquiring about acquaintances and relatives. There was no hint of the dawn excursion across the river, and the youth was stunned, upon arriving in the city a couple of hours later, to hear that the Vice-President had shot General Hamilton that very morning.

" It can't be true! " he cried. " I have just left him — he said nothing."

It was in Burr's nature to show himself composed and silent on the affair that morning, and the days that followed brought no change in his attitude. True, before Hamilton's death, he sent to Dr. Hosack to inquire about the wounded man's condition, but on the next day, he wrote to his son-in-law of his victim's death and spoke of efforts *to excite public sympathy in his favour and indignation against his antagonist.* There was no word of regret then or later to anyone. *I propose leaving town for a few days,*[57] he went on, and must have known that it would be the only course open to him, eventually.

Nine days later, fear of a murder charge and the mounting hatred with which his name was uttered in the city forced Burr to flee. At nightfall he closed the door on Richmond Hill for the last time and embarked upon the river from a wharf near the mansion.

Next morning the barge lay off the landing at Commodore Thomas Truxtun's riverside home at Perth Amboy, New Jersey, while Burr waited to learn whether his old friend would receive him. Truxtun, deploring the duel and its result, nevertheless set the fugitive on the road south in his own carriage. Using little-traveled roads and byways, Burr at last reached the Philadelphia home of Charles Biddle, where he fancied himself safe.

I walk and ride about here as usual,[58] he told Theodosia in a letter, and joked a little about his prospects in renewing a flirtation of several years' duration with a young lady of the city. His daughter would be able to find no evidence of a heavy heart in Burr's description of his situation: *If any male friend of yours should be dying of ennui, recommend to him to engage in a duel and a courtship at the same time.*[59]

The foppish little man, making his way about Philadelphia, excited more than a little curiosity. What would the Vice-President do now? it was asked. His term would end in a few months' time. He had no future in public life; he was bankrupt and charged with murder. What did the years ahead hold for Aaron Burr?

The truth of the matter was that the urbane manner and smiling countenance that Philadelphia saw concealed a desperate eagerness for the future. It was already being shaped beneath Charles Biddle's roof by Burr and another gentleman with a well-developed talent for intrigue — General James Wilkinson, who had shared the hardships of the Revolutionary march through the Maine wilderness to Quebec.

Quite simply, the future plotted by these two in the heat of late July, 1804, was treason against the United States. The nation's Vice-President and its ranking general proposed to create a splendid new empire by uniting Spain's Mexican colonies with the vast territories west of the Allegheny Mountains.

The idea was not a new one with either man. Burr had begun to eye the West as soon as it became apparent that his political fortunes were ebbing, and Wilkinson, who had become a traitor to his country when he swore allegiance to the Spanish crown in 1787, had been thinking of an expedition against Mexico for years. The unsavory alliance between the two had been born in guarded talks at Richmond Hill several weeks before the duel at Weehawken. Now they worked with feverish urgency, charting the first moves of the venture and listing the factors necessary for its success.

" There must be trouble between the United States and Spain to justify the Mexican conquest," Burr said.

" No difficulty there," his confederate replied. " Spain is in a mood to fight over the extent of the territory that Napoleon so kindly sold to Mr. Jefferson's commissioners. There will be shooting on the border before the affair is settled."

" And the people of the West will support that action, you think? "

" There's no doubt about it at all. The Dons are even
less popular in that part of the country than officials of
the Federal Government." The general paused a moment, then added, " The movement toward independence grows stronger daily."

" Yes, there will be a separation of the East and
West — it's bound to come." Burr was confident on the
point, and he was not alone in his opinion. In 1804,
many Americans believed that the barrier of the Appalachian range seemed to define a separate nation.
Settlers who, since the Revolution, had poured through
the passes into lands drained by the Ohio and Mississippi Rivers, had interests and problems that differed
completely from those of their eastern brethren. Little
help had come from Washington, and the mounting
tide of resentment against the Federal Government
was a thing upon which Burr counted heavily.

Wilkinson had been stationed in the West for many
years and thought that some military men of the frontier might be persuaded to join the venture. He would
sound them out. Naval aid was a possibility too, said
Burr. He promised to talk to Commodore Truxtun,
who was in a towering rage with Mr. Jefferson over his
forced retirement.

The knowledge that vast sums of money would be required failed to disturb Burr. One had only to apply for
funds where the success of the scheme would be most
welcome, and who would benefit more from a divided
United States than Great Britain? Charles Williamson,
a trusted friend, was delegated to broach the matter to
Anthony Merry, British Minister to Washington.

Merry listened, goggle-eyed, as Williamson gave him the Vice-President's message: "Mr. Burr is prepared to assist the British government in separating the western states from the American Union. Financial aid will be needed, and a naval force to operate at the mouth of the Mississippi." The dazed Britisher agreed that the proposal had interesting aspects. He would write to his government. Mr. Williamson might go to London to press the case personally, if he wished.

The conspirators were jubilant when they parted a few days later, Wilkinson to begin recruiting help in the West, his partner to seek asylum in the South, where the death of Alexander Hamilton was not so much regretted.

The late summer and early fall of 1804 were a pleasant interlude for Burr. Welcomed wherever he went, he had an opportunity to visit the Alstons and make the acquaintance of his two-year-old grandson, Aaron Burr Alston. As the weeks passed, he learned that the ferment of wrath raised by the duel was quieting, and by the time Congress met, he felt safe in returning to the capital to take his seat as President of the Senate.

Burr spent a busy winter, engaged by day in the nation's lawmaking procedures, while by night he plotted its destruction. Wilkinson was often in Washington to help with the copying of maps, and to report on progress in the western country. The West was indeed ripe for revolt and the conquest of Mexico, he told Burr. It could not be doubted. He had enlisted a number of important recruits, among them John Adair, a Kentuckian who was soon to be elected to the Senate. "The word is all we wait for," [60] Adair had promised upon joining the plot. The general had noted the same reaction everywhere.

Burr, too, had succeeded in making recruits, but more important were the appointments that his position had enabled him to secure. His stepson, John B. Prevost, had gone out to New Orleans as territorial judge. His good friend, James Brown, was the secretary of the New Orleans Territory. Dr. Joseph Browne, a kinsman, had been named to the same post for Louisiana Territory. And, presently, General Wilkinson learned of his appointment as governor of Louisiana.

Wilkinson and Browne will suit most admirably as eaters and laughers, and, I believe, in all other particulars,[61] Burr told Theodosia in a letter. He had no need to elaborate, for the Alstons knew his plans in detail. Indeed, Theodosia was already dreaming of herself in the splendid robes of heiress-apparent to the throne of an empire in the West.

The conspiracy did not long remain the guarded secret of a few men. Rumors concerning a plot against Louisiana began to circulate in the fall of 1804, and by spring, official Washington was whispering the names of Burr and Wilkinson. Louis Turreau, the French Minister, did not doubt the truth of the stories. *Louisiana is thus going to be the seat of Mr. Burr's new intrigues; he is going there under the aegis of General Wilkinson,* he informed his government.

Burr was, in fact, almost ready to pack his bags, as Turreau wrote. On March 2, he made a final appearance before the Senate, bidding the members farewell with grave eloquence. " This house is a sanctuary; a citadel of law, of order, and of liberty," he said, " and if the Constitution be destined ever to perish by the sacrilegious hands of the demagogue or the usurper, which God avert, its expiring agonies will be witnessed on this floor." [62]

No one could remember afterward how long he had spoken, and when he had finished, the senators watched him walk up the aisle for the last time, too moved for ordinary applause. " How can this man be thought guilty of intriguing against the nation? " they asked one another, and were persuaded that the rumors must be false. Senator Jonathan Dayton of New Jersey, Burr's college friend and present accomplice, was among the few who knew that they were not.

On April 10, 1805, Burr set out on an exploratory journey through the West. At Pittsburgh, he purchased for $113 a flatboat — a luxurious craft, sixty feet long, which boasted a kitchen with fireplace, a dining room, and two bedrooms — and began a leisurely cruise down the Ohio. It must have been a delightful journey through a spring-green wilderness unmarked by civilization, save for a few backwoods settlements.

Early in May, near Marietta, Ohio, Burr came upon an island estate, set like a jewel in the river. A magnificent house was surrounded with gardens and lawns that stretched to the water's edge. The adventurer put ashore, fascinated by the prospect of making the acquaintance of a man with money enough to create such a paradise.

Harman Blennerhassett, the Irish expatriate owner of the island retreat, was not at home, but his lovely wife welcomed the distinguished guest and invited him to dine. Burr noted the elegant furnishings of the mansion while he exerted all his charm on the lady. What a stroke of luck it would be if he could obtain a place like this, together with the wealth it represented, for a base of operations! The mistress of the house was plainly falling under his spell. Perhaps her husband would be as responsive. He left the island, fully determined to pursue the matter of friendship with Mr. Blennerhassett at the earliest opportunity.

The remainder of Burr's western journey of 1805 proved to be as pleasant as the brief stay on Blennerhassett's Island had been. Everywhere, he radiated satisfaction and goodwill as he found that men of substance were flocking to join him. In Cincinnati, there was Senator John Smith, for instance, and in Frankfort, Kentucky, which he reached by horseback, Senator John Brown. Adair, of the same state, was, of course, already pledged to Wilkinson.

On May 29, he rode into Nashville, Tennessee, and went directly to The Hermitage, home of Andrew Jackson, who had been his admirer since 1794, when the Tennessean had been the first representative to Congress from his newly admitted state. Dismounting to a hearty welcome, the visitor knew that he must guard his speech in this house. Although he hoped to have Jackson's aid eventually, such confidences as had been given to the Ohio and Kentucky people would never do. The story must be tailored, at the proper time, for the ears of a man who was made of different stuff.

Burr stayed at The Hermitage for four days and had little to say about his activities in the West, except that they had the approval of the Secretary of War.

Jackson had heard an outright lie, of course, one which was to be repeated in a variety of ways to many men. Nor was it the only falsehood that Burr produced in the course of the conspiracy. Before the affair had

ended, he was apt to tell the truth only when it served
his purpose better than a lie.

Early in June, Burr was at Fort Massac on the Ohio
for a series of earnest conferences with Wilkinson.
When they had ended, the general supplied notes of
introduction to men who might be useful in New Orleans, and once again, the traveler set out on the river
highway, bound for his most important port of call.

The slow drift down the Mississippi in June's steam-
ing heat was a time of speculation for Burr. So far, all
had gone well, but there were critical questions to be
asked in New Orleans. What sort of answers would he
get?

Pausing at Natchez, he surveyed the little settlement of three or four hundred houses with approval.
In a year's time, he decided, he would stop here with
Theodosia and, in these pleasant surroundings, await a
summons to begin his reign. First, he would hear that a
declaration of independence had been read in the New
Orleans legislature, and then, that Aaron Burr had
been named head of state by acclamation. After that,
he would enter the city, with his force supported by
Wilkinson's troops, appropriate the funds of its banks,
commandeer the ships in port, and all would be in order for the descent upon Mexico.

There need be no great concern about the other
states and territories of the Mississippi-Ohio basin,
Burr told himself. They would quickly pledge allegiance to the power that controlled the flow of ship-
ping into the Gulf of Mexico. Their interests would
compel it.

Such were the dreams of the conspirator during the
last two weeks of the river journey, and when he

landed on the levee bank at New Orleans, it appeared that they might all be realized. His welcome could not have been more enthusiastic. To the city's nine thousand inhabitants, largely of French and Spanish origin, Alexander Hamilton was a name of little consequence, and the manner of his death had not tarnished the reputation of their visitor.

Flashing the famous smile and practicing his careful French, he proceeded in triumph from one entertainment to another. The best houses in the city rang with toasts to Colonel Burr, lately Vice-President of the United States.

Meanwhile, the business of the conspiracy was going forward in meetings with some of New Orleans' most influential citizens, many of them members of the Mexican Association which for years had been dedicated to wresting Spain's Mexican colonies from her. Burr asked his questions and was assured that all would be in readiness when he came that way again. "The thing will begin in New Orleans, then," he promised, taking leave of new friends and old after three weeks. "I shall see you again next year — probably in October."

CHAPTER 10

THE FALL OF AARON
THE FIRST

ON THE RETURN JOURNEY, Burr again saw Wilkinson in St. Louis. By this time the general's enthusiasm for the plot was cooling rapidly. He had had little success in recruiting young army officers, and he was beginning to suspect that the West was not so ready for revolt as he had thought. Moreover, he was growing indignant about Burr's presumptuous attitude on the Mexican venture. "Do you not know I have reserved these places [the Mexican provinces] for my own triumphant entry, that I have been reconnoitering and exploring the route for sixteen years?" [63] he asked John Adair a short time later.

Burr sensed nothing of this during the St. Louis meeting, and rode away in ignorance of the fact that the conspiracy had begun to fall apart. The first intimations of possible failure came only after he reached Washington in mid-November to find that the Louisiana boundary dispute had simmered down, and that there had not been a single word of reply from Great Britain to his proposition.

The colonel heard the news with a sinking heart, but he rallied quickly. A declaration of war against Spain was perhaps not altogether necessary. The financial problem was another thing. He must have money. Once again, Anthony Merry heard the plan for an empire in the West outlined, this time by the would-be emperor whose suave words cloaked a threat: "The Louisianans are so impatient under American rule that they were about to send deputies to Paris when I reached New Orleans," said Burr. "I persuaded them that independence under British protection was preferable. Surely, your ministry will see the advantage of such a thing. All that will be required are two or three frigates, and a number of smaller vessels to operate in the Gulf — and a small sum of money, say about 110,-000 pounds."

Promising to write again, Merry sounded no great note of hope, and Burr took his leave, determined to fish in other waters. There was that wealthy Irishman in his Ohio River mansion, for instance. A letter was posted shortly, inviting Mr. Blennerhassett to join an exciting venture that could not fail to double or treble his investment. Son-in-law Alston, already a convert to the scheme, must be persuaded to give and give. And there were men whose claims to lands west of the Alleghenies had not been recognized by the Federal Government. They should certainly be interested in supporting a cause that would grant them clear titles.

Burr began to cast his lures, and as time went on, the words of which they were fashioned grew wilder. In fact, desperation to make the mad plan succeed may have crazed him a little. There is a strong suspicion that a deranged mind concocted the story which Jonathan Dayton, pleading for funds, told Spanish Minister Casa Yrujo: "Mr. Burr plans to get an armed force into Washington by stealth, stage a *coup d'état,* and take the President and Vice-President. He will then seize the arsenal and the Bank of the United States at Georgetown. If he cannot establish himself in Washington, he will burn the Navy Yard, with the exception of two or three ships in which he will sail to New Orleans to proclaim the independence of the West."

The same yarn, with minor variations, was to be repeated a number of times. Marine Corps General William Eaton heard it a short time later from Burr himself: " If I can gain over the Marine Corps and secure to my interests Truxtun, Decatur, and Preble [top-ranking American naval officers], I will turn Congress neck and heels out of doors, get rid of the President, and declare myself protector of the Government."

Benjamin Stoddert, who had been the first Secretary of the Navy in the Adams administration, remembered later that Burr had talked wildly of a *coup d'état.* " With five hundred men, I could send Jefferson to Monticello and put myself at the head of the Government," he had asserted, according to Stoddert.

Truxtun was approached in a more temperate fashion, however, and Burr alluded, for the first time, to a new element in the plot — his recent purchase of a huge portion of the Ouachita land grant in Louisiana. " In case of a war with Spain, I shall make an attack on Mexico by way of Veracruz," said Burr, and hinted that the Government backed his plan.

" There will be no war," Truxtun assured him.

" In that case, I shall settle the Ouachita lands and wait my chance."

Truxtun quizzed his visitor sharply on the Government's involvement, and upon gaining an admission that there was none, closed the interview with a flat, " I am not interested."

Things were going very badly for Burr. He knew that if Truxtun could not be enlisted, it would be useless to try his wiles on Captains Decatur and Preble. Furthermore, he had not heard from Wilkinson in months, and there was still no word on possible foreign aid. Merry continued to be regretful when asked about news from London, and Yrujo had failed to pledge his government for more than a few hundred dollars. (The shrewd Spaniard never intended to do more than keep the line of communication open.)

Prospects for the conspiracy's success were sorry indeed during the winter of 1805–1806. But as the days began to lengthen, the picture brightened perceptibly. Trouble was again brewing on the southwestern border (Surely, Wilkinson can stir that up somehow, thought Burr), and money was coming to hand. Blennerhassett, dazzled by the honor of associating with such celebrated company, had agreed to commit the whole of his resources. Alston was contributing huge amounts, and the funds collected from eager investors were swelling.

In May, Burr was his usual arrogant self when he paid Merry a last call. " The disposition of the inhabitants of the western country, and particularly Louisiana, to separate themselves from the American Union is so strong that the attempt might be made with every prospect of success without any foreign assistance whatever," [64] he told the British envoy.

July saw him winding up affairs in the East and writing, in cipher, a last batch of lies to Wilkinson: *Naval*

*protection of England is secured. Truxtun is going to
Jamaica to arrange with the admiral on that station.
It [a squadron] will meet us at the Mississippi. England, a navy of the United States, are ready to
join. . . . Burr will proceed westward first August,
never to return.*[65] The intriguer went on to say that he
would meet his partner at Natchez between the fifth
and fifteenth of December, and concluded this monu-
mental fabrication by asserting, *The people of the
country to which we are going are prepared to receive
us. . . . In three weeks all will be settled. The gods in-
vite us to glory and fortune.*[66]

Ready at last to accept the invitation, Burr was in
Pittsburgh in mid-August, arranging transport for the
hundreds of young men, enlisted by his confederates,
who would shortly rendezvous there.

He was still recruiting wherever he saw the opportunity, and remembered that a college classmate living
nearby had sons who might be persuaded to join him.
He decided to call on Colonel George Morgan. The
colonel welcomed the friend of Princeton days warmly,
but his smile faded at hints of the business afoot in the
West, and he sickened with dread when Burr ended a
tirade against Jefferson with the oft-repeated threat:
" With two hundred men, I could drive the President
and Congress into the Potomac." [67]

The visitor was not long in realizing that he had
made his boast to the wrong man, but he was not
greatly worried. The project had been set in motion —
nothing could stop it now. A few days later, he landed
at Blennerhassett's Island for a first meeting with the
man who was to play so large a part in the undertaking.

Theodosia joined him there, and together they exulted over the Irishman's report that everything was going splendidly. Expedition boats ordered locally were nearing completion, and the island was being prepared as a supply depot for the final push.

When Blennerhassett asked, " What else can I do to help? " his chief was prompt with an answer: " You can enlist public support in this area."

A short time after Burr's departure from the island, the Marietta newspaper began publication of a series of articles signed *Querist*. The gist of the pieces: The West was being exploited by eastern commercial interests. The only solution to the difficulty lay in the separation of the two sections.

A few of Blennerhassett's neighbors heard him identify himself as the author, and they were horrified to learn that he and Mr. Burr proposed to bring about that separation very shortly. Again the fanatic words (a clear echo of Burr) were voiced: " If Federal officials in Washington make any trouble, they will be thrown into the Potomac."

Unknowingly, Burr had long been sowing seeds of disaster. While he was bustling about, making his final preparations on the Ohio, men who had had his confidences were talking. Truxtun, forgetting his differences with Jefferson, had reported the proposition made to him. So, too, had General Eaton. Information had reached Washington on Burr's recruiting activities in Pennsylvania and New York, and Colonel George Morgan's warnings of peril to the nation were so frantic that he was at first thought to be out of his mind.

The seed that flourished best, however, was the one sown by the *Querist* articles. Jefferson, at last aroused to the immediate danger, sent an agent west to find out what his ex-Vice-President was up to, and in Kentucky, a young Federal attorney, who had long been eyeing Burr's comings and goings with suspicion, resolved to act. Early in November, he asked for a grand jury investigation of the conspiracy that was now on everyone's lips.

Accompanied by attorney Henry Clay, Burr appeared in court at Frankfort, Kentucky, but the young prosecutor had been in too much haste. The inquiry must be postponed until witnesses could be located. Colonel Burr was excused for the moment.

The legal action taken against him must have made it clear to the conspirator that the real objectives of the plot were too widely known, for from that time forward, his tune changed significantly. People began to hear only about plans for the colonization of the Ouachita lands — the colonel was offering cash, tools, and seed to settlers. When twenty-nine-year-old Henry Clay grew suspicious and demanded to know his client's true purposes in the West, Burr assured him that he had no designs against the United States, " did not own, nor did anyone own for him, any single item of military stores."

He was sufficiently successful in masking his intentions, so that when he was again summoned to Frankfort, the Grand Jury could " discover nothing improper or injurious to the interest of the Government of the United States " in the ex-Vice-President's conduct.

Even as the verdict was being read, boats were being loaded at Blennerhassett's Island for the long trip to New Orleans, and the Governor of Ohio, fully informed on the conspiracy by Jefferson's agent, was issuing orders to seize any that could be found.

Andrew Jackson, too, had had his eyes opened by a story whose reliability he could not doubt. It had been reported to him that one of Burr's friends claimed that he intended to split the Union. " I will die in the last ditch before I would . . . see the Union disunited," [68] vowed the man who was to be its seventh president.

A short time after his acquittal in Frankfort, Burr arrived in Nashville. Jackson stormed into his lodgings and flung the story at him. " No, no! Upon my honor, I have the approval of the Government! " cried the man who had forgotten that the words " honor " and " honesty " have a common Latin root. He rummaged through a bundle of papers and produced a blank commission, signed *Thomas Jefferson*. " I suppose this will satisfy you! "

Confused by his one-time friend's manner and the pilfered document, Jackson turned over to him two of the five flatboats promised earlier, and Burr set off down the Cumberland River for his rendezvous with glory and fortune.

Five days later, on December 27, Blennerhassett, waiting at an island in the Ohio with a sorry little flotilla of eight boats, hailed his commander in chief. Threats of a militia raid had forced him to flee by night from the trampled mire of his once lovely estate, he confessed. The other boats had all been lost — seized on the river or in the boatyard.

Burr swallowed his disappointment. There might be only a handful of men now, but hundreds, gathering at various points on the Ohio, would follow, and his general was waiting at the scene of action. The expedition continued on down the Ohio and into the Mississippi,

the colonel recruiting at every landing with all the persuasion at his command. Enlistees were now offered
$12.50 a month. Frontier post army officers, urged to
resign their commissions and join up, heard the well-
rehearsed repertoire of lies: The Government was behind Colonel Burr's project. Wilkinson's force was to
be committed to him. General Eaton was on his way
with the Navy. Only a few men answered Burr's call to
arms, but he contrived to maintain an air of confident
assurance as the little fleet drifted downriver.

Then, on Saturday morning, January 10, the dream
world of Emperor Aaron the First was blown apart
with a suddenness that must have left the dreamer
reeling. Thirty miles from Natchez, he halted at a
small riverside settlement to call upon an old friend,
who thrust at him a newspaper that spelled out the
end of the conspiracy: There was a presidential proc-
lamation condemning the expedition. Orders for Burr's
arrest had been issued in the Mississippi Territory.
And Wilkinson, who had abandoned the project
months earlier unbeknownst to Burr, was now boast-
ing that he would seize the villain who threatened his
beloved country.

The way to New Orleans was closed. The turncoat,
playing the hero soldier there, was arresting agents of
the conspiracy right and left. In order to escape the
summary military justice that he might expect if he
were taken by his former partner, Burr agreed to surrender to territorial officers. The atmosphere in Mississippi was not unfriendly to a man who said he intended nothing but action against the hated Spanish,
and a grand jury, meeting on February 2, failed to find
the colonel guilty of anything.

However, the court would not release him from his bond, and an armed party, sent by Wilkinson to abduct him, was said to be in the vicinity. Burr realized that the time for flight had come. By night, he crossed the river to the Louisiana shore, where his sad little fleet was waiting, and put an end to the great adventure. " I have been acquitted, but they mean to take me again, and I am forced to flee from oppression," [69] he told the downcast little group of followers. " I have nothing to give you, but you may sell the boats and stores, and go to the Ouachita lands, if you like." With those words of farewell, Aaron Burr, a fugitive from justice, took to his heels.

Mounted on a shabby horse, and disguised in frontiersman's garb, with a knife in his belt and a tin can hanging from his shoulder, he and a single companion sought the wilderness trails that led to safety across the southeastern border of the United States. The pair escaped notice for more than two weeks before a villager, from whom directions were asked, became curious about the oddly silent man whose hat brim hid his face. " I think it was Aaron Burr," he told the commanding officer at a nearby fort. Arrested on the trail the following morning, the fugitive shortly began the long journey to Richmond, Virginia, that was to end in his trial for high treason against the United States.

The spring of 1807 gave way to summer while Burr remained under lock and key, and witnesses paraded into the hall of Virginia's House of Delegates to tell their stories to a grand jury. In Washington, President Jefferson waited impatiently for the indictment that must result, and when it was announced, he was certain that the outcome of Burr's trial would be a verdict of guilty. The President reckoned without the presiding judge, Chief Justice John Marshall of the United States Supreme Court.

For almost a month in the heat of late summer, Marshall and the jury listened to the details of the Burr Conspiracy and examined the few available notes and letters that had been exchanged by the intriguers. The witnesses were in no doubt about the colonel's purposes, but the written evidence might be interpreted as having to do solely with the conquest of Mexico. That would have been a crime, of course, but it was not the one for which a conviction was sought.

Meanwhile, the accused man and his attorneys continued to claim that he had committed no act of treason. No matter if Colonel Burr was thought to have planned to do this or that, said the defense. The real point was that he personally had not lifted a finger against the United States.

In rendering his opinion to the jury, Marshall agreed. According to Article III, Section 3, of the Constitution, *Treason against the United States shall consist only in levying war against them,* and going to war must *be proven by open deeds.* Concluding an opinion that required three hours in the reading, the Chief Justice said that no overt act of treason by the defendant had been established during the trial.

Twenty-five minutes after he turned the case over to the jury, a verdict of " Not Guilty " was returned to the courtroom, and Aaron Burr was again free to pursue his insane hopes for the future.

CHAPTER 11

THE EXILE

DURING THE CAPTIVE MARCH to justice, Aaron Burr, still in his wretched disguise, had been bitterly humiliated, but his shame had disappeared with the rags. Supported by Theodosia's devoted presence, and surrounded by Federalist legal talent, which sought as much to injure Jefferson as to help the defendant, Burr had gone into court once again the cocky, assured man of affairs.

Harman Blennerhassett, also under arrest in Richmond, was astonished and resentful when he visited the man whose wild notions of empire had cost him everything he owned. He found Burr enjoying comfort, even luxury, in his penitentiary quarters, and " as gay as usual."

What right had he to put on such a face? the defrauded Irishman wondered, and was silent when the conspirator remarked that in six months all their schemes could be remounted. " I shall not lose a day after the favorable issue here, of which I have no doubt, to direct my entire attention to setting my projects on a better model," said Burr. " Even here I have made some progress, and I mean to go to England once this business is done."

Within a few weeks of acquittal, the colonel had another reason for leaving the country. He must do so to save his skin from tar and feathers, it seemed. Lawyers may have convinced the jury in Richmond, but they had failed with the nation, which still called the little man a traitor. Barely escaping the attentions of a mob in Baltimore, he hid with friends while arranging for his flight, and early in June, 1808, after a tearful parting from his daughter, he sailed for England.

Burr realized shortly after his arrival in London that he would have no easy time in " setting his projects on a better model." Spain was now an ally of Great Britain, and the disposition of her Mexican colonies was not a timely subject for discussion in government circles. The King's ministers turned him away coldly, hinting that he might not long be welcome in their country.

The threat of expulsion brought forth a shocking response: " I demand my right to live in England on the ground that I was born and still remain a British subject," said the man who had served four years in the Revolution, and had been elected to the second highest office in the United States. Burr never lived down this claim which one of the ministers termed " monstrous."

Money was always a problem for the exile. Theodosia's failure to collect old debts forced him to economize for the first time in his life, and he considered it a most fortunate thing for his purse that British intellectuals welcomed him to their homes and tables.

Philosopher Jeremy Bentham was the warmest of the new friends, and Burr confided in him as he had in few other men. " He really meant to make himself Emperor of Mexico," said Bentham long afterward, " and if his project had failed in Mexico, he meant to set up for a monarch in the United States." On the subject of Hamilton's death, Burr told him that he had gone to the dueling ground sure of being able to kill him. " I thought it little better than a murder," said the philosopher, but his friendship did not waver.

The fruitless weeks dragged into months, and at year's end, to divert himself, if not to seek new allies, Burr set off on a tour of the country. When he returned to London in February, 1809, empty of pocket and hopeless, he learned that he was about to be arrested for debt. He went into hiding as Mr. Kirby.

By this time, the British Government had had enough of sheltering a man who had been hounded from the shores of the American Republic. There was sufficient trouble brewing across the Atlantic without that. Agents located Mr. Kirby promptly, and in April, still protesting " the rights which, as a natural-born subject, he might legally assert," he was bundled off to Sweden.

The five-month visit to Sweden was pleasant. Burr had never known weather so uniformly fine, and he found the Swedes sensitive, generous, and likable. Nevertheless, he knew that he must move on — there was no future for him in Stockholm. He must make his way somehow to the one man in Europe powerful enough to bring his dreams to life — Napoleon Bonaparte, Emperor of the French.

In the fall of 1809, he left Sweden and crossing Denmark, traveled slowly through Germany, embarrassed, as always, where his pocketbook was concerned. At one point, he was so destitute that he was obliged to pawn his pencil to pay a bridge toll. But the distinction of having been Vice-President of the United States, and his fascinating manners were enough for the nobility of the principalities he visited. Colonel Burr was royally entertained.

In fact, in Weimar, he almost became a permanent addition to the court when a flirtation with a lovely lady of rank became a serious thing. Burr, who never missed a pretty face and apparently left broken hearts wherever he went, was ready to make a proposal that he was sure would be accepted. At the last moment he changed his mind.

Another interview, and I might have been lost, he wrote Theodosia, *my hopes and projects blasted and abandoned. The horror of this last catastrophe struck me so forcibly, and the danger was so imminent, that at eight o'clock I ordered posthorses, gave a crown extra to the postillion to drive like the devil, and lo! here I am safely locked within the walls of Erfurth, rejoicing and repining.*[70]

The visa necessary for entry into France was obtained after several delays, and Burr reached Paris early in 1810, afire with renewed hope. Napoleon had lately agreed that Spain's American colonies ought to be independent, and surely could be convinced that Colonel Burr's carefully laid plans deserved support.

While he scurried about the city by day, trying to gain the ears of the imperial ministers, Burr labored by night on a message for His Majesty. Filling page after page with painstaking French, the intriguer outlined the elements of the conspiracy that had first been drafted in Philadelphia in the winter of 1805. He pic-

tured the United States as a nation ruined by the policies of its presidents, restless and dissatisfied. Louisiana, he said, was ready for separation. He knew that
from his own observations in New Orleans: *About
three years go I saw a memorial already signed by a
number of inhabitants, in which they set forth their
grievances and implored your protection.*[71]

This was only one of the circumstances noted, said
Burr, *indicating that a change in the United States and
the English colonies is not distant.* He continued with
a pair of sly inquiries: *Is not Your Majesty interested
in taking part in this great event? Will you leave it to
chance?* [72]

Conditions favored a war between the United States
and Great Britain, he claimed (the Emperor would not
miss the hint that he could be helpful in provoking
that), and all the aid that Burr required in addition
was a frigate or two, and some smaller vessels. He
could obtain and man a number of merchant vessels
with disgruntled American seamen, of whom there
was no lack. He could count, too, on support from the
Tennessee, Ohio, and Cumberland districts of the Mississippi, said Burr.

The document, preserved in the French National
Archives, appears to set the seal on Aaron Burr's guilt
of disloyalty to his country, for this is a treasonous
proposal to a foreign power, written boldly in ink that
has not faded in more than a century and a half.

Napoleon probably never saw it, for it is filed with a
tightly written three-page analysis which must have
been prepared for his attention. The man who was
given the task of editing Aaron Burr's splendid words
and phrases was often puzzled. In a parenthetical

comment, he wrote, *The author seems sooner to wish to be guessed at, than to explain himself openly. It seems that he is the head of a third party which tends toward monarchy.*[73]

Perhaps the intimation that the petitioner was power hungry, too, cooled Napoleon's interest in Aaron Burr. In any case, no word of acknowledgment was accorded the extraordinary document, and five months later, Burr was finally obliged to admit to himself that his dreams of empire must die.

It was time to seek the quiet private life that he had abandoned so many years before, time to go home again — if the homeland would have him — to embrace Theodosia and the beloved grandson who would be a great boy now, almost nine years old.

However, leaving France was to be no easier for Aaron Burr than gaining entry had been. His political enemies, wishing to see no more of the man, had persuaded the French not to let him go.

The exile considered his circumstances with wry humor. *Behold me, a prisoner of state, and almost without a soul!*[74] he scrawled in his journal. Seeking the means of survival, he borrowed where he could, and sold many of the gifts intended for Theodosia and the boy. Often, during the months that followed, he was cold and hungry while he went the rounds of officialdom, begging for the documents he needed.

A full year passed before they were granted, but even then, Burr's troubles had not ended. The American ship in which he sailed from Holland had not been a day at sea before being seized and interned by the British. Stranded in London, his passage money lost, he spent the next six months in a desperate search for

funds and a ship to carry him home. The meager pos-
sessions remaining to him disappeared, one by one,
and he was truly penniless when he reached New York
in June, 1812, after four years of exile.

Uncertain of the nature of his welcome, believing
that immediate arrest was a real threat, he crept into
the city by night and sought refuge with friends. He
had left the country under bond to appear for trial in
Ohio, the old indictments for murder had never been
quashed, and there were creditors by the score who
might drag him into court. Burr dared to show himself
only after it became clear that the news of his return
had been accepted with indifference. In those first
weeks of the war with Great Britain that he had fore-
seen, the nation had larger concerns than the revival
of an old scandal.

Late in the summer, there was a brief announcement
in a New York newspaper: *Aaron Burr has returned
to the city and has resumed the practice of the law in
Nassau Street.*[75] Clients flocked to the little office, eager
to avail themselves of a famous legal talent, and again
Burr was buoyant with confidence. The future still
promised much for a vigorous man in his fifties, he told
himself. He would pay his debts, might even yet be
rich, and he would see his own dreams fulfilled in the
lives of his idolized daughter and grandson.

Before a year had passed, Aaron Burr knew that
nothing but lonely old age lay ahead. All that he had
lived for was gone. Theodosia and her son were both
dead, the boy of a fever, his mother lost at sea on a
voyage from Charleston to New York.

Drained of personal ambition, he lived for twenty-
three years after the double tragedy, seldom heard

from or seen except in the courts of law.

It was a period of dramatic development for the Republic which he had thought to dominate, and although he was isolated from public affairs, Burr followed them with keen interest.

Seventeen states had made up the Union when he sailed into exile. The eighteenth, Louisiana, was admitted while he was at sea on the voyage home, and in the following decade, six more, Indiana, Mississippi, Illinois, Alabama, Maine, and Missouri, joined the Federal partnership. Virtually all the country upon which Aaron Burr had once cast a designing eye had thus committed itself to the Republic. He must have been sharp enough to see that he had completely mistaken the temper of those western men. Moreover, the opening of new roads and canals, and the advent of steam locomotion in 1825 made it clear that the barriers of distance and a mountain range, which he had once thought so important, were no longer significant. The spirit of union was keeping pace with the advancing frontier.

Presidents Madison and Monroe, under whom the United States had discovered a national pride, earned no word of praise from the old man, however. They had been his political enemies, and he held them both in contempt. Monroe, in particular, he considered a very " dull fellow," although the President's message of 1823, the statement of the Monroe Doctrine, warning European powers not " to extend their system to any portion of this hemisphere," must have entitled him to a nod, at the very least.

After his return from exile, New York never really accepted Aaron Burr, except in a professional capacity.

As the years passed, young men joined their fathers in avoiding his glance when they met him in the streets, and he knew that the odium attached to his name was growing rather than diminishing with time.

Burr's story became a legend of villainy while he lived, and when he grew quite old, his shrunken figure, brown face, and bright, dark eyes made him the very picture of evil for the children who played in his street. " Some terrible old man lives there alone, and nobody will speak to him," they said, pointing to his house. If Burr knew this, he must have been terribly hurt, for he had always loved children.

In the last years before his death, the past seemed to occupy his thoughts more than the sad present. The people of Princeton grew accustomed to seeing him visit and walk through the town and pause a moment to look at Nassau Hall and the president's house, before going on to the cemetery where parents and grandparents lay. Each time, they thought that he must soon join them — he looked so fragile under his huge, rusty top hat.

Burr's few friends continued to marvel at his vigor and the serenity and composure with which he bore himself. They reflected that in only one way did he resemble the old Burr. He still spent his money as fast as he got it, and he never ran out of ideas for making himself rich. He was seventy-seven when he amazed them by marrying a wealthy widow of rather tarnished reputation whose splendid home no doubt recalled the elegance of Richmond Hill. Strolling in the pleasant grounds of the mansion on Harlem Heights must have evoked even earlier memories. Here, George Washington had made his headquarters during the battle for Manhattan Island nearly sixty years before.

The marriage did not last long, the second Mrs. Burr sending her husband packing when she discovered that he was going through her fortune with incredible speed.

A short time later, his health began to fail, and in the summer of 1836, when he was eighty years old, it became apparent that Aaron Burr's life was about to end. A friend asked, for the last time, the question to which there had never been a satisfactory answer: Had he really intended a division of the Union with his expedition of thirty years before?

A falsehood oft-repeated over the years tends to become the truth in an old man's mind, and there is little doubt that Aaron Burr went to his grave in Princeton Cemetery, believing his last, sincere protestation of innocence: " I would as soon have thought of taking possession of the moon, and informing my friends that I intended to divide it among them! " [76]

NOTES

1. Nathan Schachner, *Aaron Burr: A Biography*, p. 16, quoting from Esther Burr's diary.
2. James Parton, *The Life and Times of Aaron Burr*, p. 62.
3. Matthew L. Davis, *Memoirs of Aaron Burr*, Vol. I, p. 46, Edwards to Burr, February 11, 1774.
4. *Ibid.*, p. 52, Burr to Ogden, March 12, 1775.
5. *Ibid.*, p. 49, Burr to Ogden, September 11, 1774.
6. *Ibid.*
7. Schachner, *Aaron Burr: A Biography*, p. 41.
8. *Ibid.*, p. 42.
9. *Ibid.*, p. 44.
10. Davis, *Memoirs of Aaron Burr*, Vol. I, p. 109, Burr to Ogden, March 7, 1777.
11. *Ibid.*
12. *Ibid.*, p. 111, Burr to Washington, July 21, 1777.
13. *Ibid.*, p. 112.
14. *Ibid.*, p. 116, Letter of Lieutenant Robert Hunter, January 22, 1814.
15. Bruce Lancaster, *From Lexington to Liberty*, p. 349.
16. *Ibid.*
17. *Ibid.*, p. 350.
18. Samuel H. Wandell and Meade Minnegerode, *Aaron Burr*, Vol. I, p. 72.
19. Lancaster, *From Lexington to Liberty*, p. 354.
20. *Ibid.*
21. Davis, *Memoirs of Aaron Burr*, Vol. I, p. 187, Paterson

to Burr, September 29, 1779.

22. *Ibid.*, pp. 192–193, Troup to Burr, February 14, 1780.

23. *Ibid.*, p. 170, Paterson to Burr, March 18, 1779.

24. *Ibid.*, p. 231, Burr to Chief Justice Morris, October 21, 1781.

25. Schachner, *Aaron Burr: A Biography*, p. 79.

26. Davis, *Memoirs of Aaron Burr*, Vol. I, p. 408.

27. *Ibid.*, p. 409.

28. Schachner, *Aaron Burr: A Biography*, p. 136.

29. Davis, *Memoirs of Aaron Burr*, Vol. I, p. 317, Burr to Theodosia, October 8, 1792.

30. *Ibid.*, pp. 373, 372, Burr to Theodosia, January 14 and 8, 1794.

31. *Ibid.*, p. 371, Burr to Theodosia, January 7, 1794.

32. Davis, *Memoirs of Aaron Burr*, Vol. II, p. 55, Jefferson to Madison, March 4, 1800.

33. *Ibid.*

34. *Ibid.*, p. 56.

35. *Ibid.*

36. *Ibid.*, p. 57.

37. Schachner, *Aaron Burr: A Biography*, p. 170.

38. *Ibid.*, pp. 176–177.

39. *Ibid.*, p. 184.

40. Wandell and Minnegerode, *Aaron Burr*, Vol. I, p. 198.

41. Schachner, *Aaron Burr: A Biography*, p. 190, Burr to Jefferson, December 23, 1800.

42. Davis, *Memoirs of Aaron Burr*, Vol. II, p. 75, Burr to Samuel Smith, December 16, 1800.

43. Schachner, *Aaron Burr: A Biography*, p. 192, from Gouverneur Morris' diary.

44. *Ibid.*, Robert G. Harper to Burr, December 24, 1800.

45. *Ibid.*, p. 193, Hamilton to Oliver Wolcott, December 16, 1800.

46. Parton, *The Life and Times of Aaron Burr*, p. 272, James A. Bayard to Hamilton, January 7, 1801.

47. Davis, *Memoirs of Aaron Burr*, Vol. II, p. 285, Burr to Theodosia, May 1, 1804.

48. Schachner, *Aaron Burr: A Biography*, p. 247.

49. Parton, *The Life and Times of Aaron Burr*, p. 339.

50. Schachner, *Aaron Burr: A Biography*, p. 247.

51. Davis, *Memoirs of Aaron Burr*, Vol. II, p. 295.

52. Harold C. Syrett and Jean G. Cooke, eds., *Interview in Weehawken*, pp. 56, 58.

53. Davis, *Memoirs of Aaron Burr*, Vol. II, p. 305.

54. Syrett and Cooke, *Interview in Weehawken*, p. 133.

55. *Ibid.*, p. 136.

56. Davis, *Memoirs of Aaron Burr*, Vol. II, p. 315.

57. *Ibid.*, p. 327.

58. *Ibid.*, p. 331.

59. *Ibid.*, p. 332.

60. Thomas Perkins Abernethy, *The Burr Conspiracy*, p. 20, John Adair to Wilkinson, December 10, 1804.

61. Davis, *Memoirs of Aaron Burr*, Vol. II, p. 360, Burr to Theodosia, March 10, 1804.

62. *Ibid.*, p. 362.

63. Abernethy, *The Burr Conspiracy*, pp. 45–46.

64. *Ibid.*, p. 56.

65. Schachner, *Aaron Burr: A Biography*, pp. 322–323.

66. *Ibid.*, p. 323.

67. Walter F. McCaleb, *The Aaron Burr Conspiracy*, p. 76.

68. *Ibid.*, p. 171.

69. *Ibid.*, p. 232.

70. Parton, *The Life and Times of Aaron Burr*, p. 548.

71. National Archives of France, AF IV 1681A, first dossier.

72. *Ibid.*

73. *Ibid.*

74. Parton, *The Life and Times of Aaron Burr*, p. 555.

75. Schachner, *Aaron Burr: A Biography*, p. 496.

76. Davis, *Memoirs of Aaron Burr*, Vol. II, p. 379.

BIBLIOGRAPHY

Abernethy, Thomas Perkins, *The Burr Conspiracy*. Oxford University Press, 1954.

Barck, Oscar Theodore, Jr., Wakefield, Walter L., and Lefler, Hugh Talmage, *The United States: A Survey of National Development*. The Ronald Press Company, 1950.

Beard, Charles A., and Mary, *A Basic History of the United States*. Doubleday & Company, Inc., 1944.

Bliven, Bruce, Jr., *Battle for Manhattan*. Henry Holt & Co., Inc., 1956.

Bowers, Claude G., *Jefferson in Power*. Houghton Mifflin Company, 1936.

Burr, Aaron, *The Private Journals of Aaron Burr*. Genesee Press, 1903.

Carman, Harry J., and Syrett, Harold C., *A History of the American People*, 2 vols. Alfred A. Knopf, Inc., 1952.

Carroll, Mary Tarver, *The Man Who Would Not Wait*. Longmans, Green & Company, Inc., 1941.

Clinton, Sir Henry, *The American Rebellion: Sir Henry Clinton's Narrative of His Campaigns, 1775–1782*, ed. by William B. Wilcox. Yale University Press, 1954.

Collins, V. Lansing, *Princeton Past and Present*. Princeton University Press, 1945.

Crouse, Anna Erskine, and Russel, *Alexander Hamilton and Aaron Burr*. Random House, Inc., 1958.

Davis, Matthew L., *Memoirs of Aaron Burr* with Miscellaneous Selections from His Correspondence, 2 vols.

Harper & Brothers, 1837.

Hacker, Louis M., *Alexander Hamilton in the American Tradition*. McGraw-Hill Book Company, Inc., 1957.

Lancaster, Bruce, *From Lexington to Liberty*. Doubleday & Company, Inc., 1955.

McCaleb, Walter F., *The Aaron Burr Conspiracy*. Dodd, Mead & Company, Inc., 1903.

Morison, Samuel Eliot, *The Oxford History of the American People*. Oxford University Press, 1965.

Morison, Samuel Eliot, and Commager, Henry Steele, *The Growth of the American Republic*, Vol. 1. Oxford University Press, 1962.

National Archives of France, AF IV 1681A, first dossier.

Norris, Edwin M., *The Story of Princeton*. Little, Brown and Company, 1917.

Parton, James, *The Life and Times of Aaron Burr*. Mason Brothers, 1863.

Peckham, Howard H., *The War for Independence: A Military History*. The University of Chicago Press, 1958.

Rankin, Hugh F., *The American Revolution*. G. P. Putnam's Sons, 1925.

Roberts, Kenneth, ed., *March to Quebec: Journals of the Members of Arnold's Expedition*. Doubleday, Doran & Company, Inc., 1938.

Schachner, Nathan, *Aaron Burr: A Biography*. Frederick A. Stokes Company, 1937.

Syrett, Harold C., and Cooke, Jean G., eds., *Interview in Weehawken: The Burr-Hamilton Duel as Told in the Original Documents*. Wesleyan University Press, 1960.

Wandell, Samuel H., and Minnegerode, Meade, *Aaron Burr*. G. P. Putnam's Sons, 1925.

BIOGRAPHY OF HELEN ORLOB

HELEN ORLOB has written many books about the sea, and she has a son who is an officer in the U.S. Navy. Born in Seattle, Washington, she graduated from the University of Washington and taught English and history in high schools in the State of Washington — a dual interest that is reflected in her skillful writing style and her keen sense of history. She has written six books for young people, one of which won the Pacific Northwest Booksellers Award for the Best Book in the Young Readers' Division in 1964.

INDEX